ENDORSEMENT

On numerous occasions I have invited Joe Smith to speak for us at Victorious Life Church in Wesley Chapel, Florida. His rich understanding, life experience and keen spiritual insight cause the scriptures to come alive to his listeners. An important part of Joe's ministry is his ability to present the word of God so that it applies to the whole man Spirit, soul and body. His teaching on this subject God in 3-D will bring a greater measure of freedom to the readers because Jesus said you will know the truth and the truth will set you free.

Ed Russo
Lead Pastor of Victorious Life Church

GOD *in* 3D

JOSEPH E SMITH

WestBow
PRESS
A DIVISION OF THOMAS NELSON

WestBow Press books may be ordered through booksellers or by contacting:

WestBow Press
A Division of Thomas Nelson
1663 Liberty Drive
Bloomington, IN 47403
www.westbowpress.com
1-(866) 928-1240

Because of the dynamic nature of the Internet, any web addresses or links contained in this book may have changed since publication and may no longer be valid. The views expressed in this work are solely those of the author and do not necessarily reflect the views of the publisher, and the publisher hereby disclaims any responsibility for them.

Any people depicted in stock imagery provided by Thinkstock are models, and such images are being used for illustrative purposes only.

Certain stock imagery © Thinkstock.

ISBN: 978-1-4497-6590-3 (sc)
ISBN: 978-1-4497-6591-0 (hc)
ISBN: 978-1-4497-6621-4 (e)

Library of Congress Control Number: 2012916432

Scripture taken from New King James Version Bible © 1979 by Thomas Nelson, Inc. Unless noted otherwise.

Printed in the United States of America

WestBow Press rev. date: 9/6/2012

CONTENTS

ACKNOWLEDGMENT

I wish to acknowledge my wife Katie who has been a constant helpmate in reading and making suggestions for improvement.

Joshua and Melissa Weber
who edited the first manuscript.

Dr. Rick Austin who edited the final manuscript.

My Pastor Ed Russo who endorsed and encouraged me in this project

INTRODUCTION

How would you answer the question, "Who is God"?

I am going to limit this book to the essential 3 D's of Scriptural truths as to who and what God is because there are untold numbers of books on the subject of God. If you can wrap your mind around these truths you will be well on your way to knowing God rather than knowing about God.

The first question in the Westminster Shorter Catechism is; what is the chief end of man? The answer is: The chief end of man is to give God glory and enjoy Him forever. The fourth question is; what is God? The answer is: God is a Spirit, infinite, eternal, and unchangeable in His being, wisdom, power, holiness, justice, goodness, and truth.

The first attribute of God, we learn from Scripture, is that God is the Creator of all things both visible and invisible. It is the visible universe that makes us aware there could be an unseen world and that life's purpose goes beyond being born, going to school, growing up, getting married, obtaining a job, retiring, and then dying. Furthermore we are impressed to believe that we should enjoy a life free from pain, sorrow, sickness, and disease. In short a life that is peaceful, tranquil, and full of joy.

Thus mankind is constantly in search for answers to what life is all about. The most common questions are about God and the spiritual dimension of life. Consequently we have 4200 religions in the world all claiming to know the answers and they cannot all be right.

Although life is a complex and sometimes bewildering experience, there are sound and realistic answers for the existence of God, our existence and purpose. These answers are found in a collection of 66 books written by 40 authors over a period of 1500 years. These books are combined into one book called the Bible. The purpose of the Bible is God revealing the process of making Him known in order that we can know Him.

In this book I will explore God and life from those authors' perspective as their books are the only true sources available to us.

FIRST D

ONE

Does God Exist?

There are many in this world who believe in the existence of God and a spiritual dimension that transcends our natural and physical world while many others reject these ideas. It stands to reason that both viewpoints cannot be right. I interpret this to mean that there are many sincere people who have no clue about who God is or if He really exists.

Various polls indicate that over 90 percent of Americans believe God exists and that there is basically no difference in the moral beliefs and actions of those who claim to know God and those who do not. Thus we have confusion in regard to the subject of God.

The reality of having forty-two-hundred religions in the world indicates that mankind, as a whole believes there is more to this world than what is seen and known from a natural, physical, and scientific perspective. This truth is also born out by cultural anthropologists who tell us there has never been a culture discovery in which the people did not have some type of religious practice.

Bertrand Russell, the renowned atheist said, "Unless you assume a God, the question of life's purpose is meaningless." I find this to be a very accurate and truthful statement.

If there is no God—there is no creation.

If there is no God—everything is by chance and not design.

If there is no God—there are no absolutes.

If there is no God—there is no right or wrong.

If there is no God—there is no life beyond our time here on earth.

If there is no God—there are no moral principles to govern how we live and treat one another.

I remember riding to work one day with an engineer who was upset over a U.S. Senator having sex with a page who worked for him. Knowing he did not believe in the existence of God I saw this as an opportunity to challenge his philosophy and asked him, "What's wrong with that?"

He seemed shocked at my question and said, "What do you mean what's wrong with that?"

"If the senator thinks its okay then what's the problem," I asked?

This really set him off and he proceeded to tell me how it was morally wrong for the senator to take advantage of a young page who worked for him. When he finished I asked him where his idea that something is right or wrong came from.

He almost yelled at me when he said, "I know what you're trying to do. You want me to say"—God—", and I'm not going to do it."

One of the main issues with God's existence and creating all that is seen and unseen is our lack of experience and observation of anything self-existing, eternal, having no beginning or end, and existing outside of time.

The universe, however, is proof that God exists. If God did not create the universe we are faced with the dilemma that nothing cannot produce anything. Thus, for anything to exist that did not previously exist, must have been *caused* to exist for it could not have created itself.

Moses wrote in Genesis that time began when God created the universe. Therefore, God exists outside of time and is not subject to time as He created time. Thus, He has no beginning or ending, for without time, there is no beginning or ending.

Another obvious truth is that if God does exist He is invisible. The fact that God is invisible leads some to doubt the existence of God. Scientists, however, have discovered many things that exist which the eye cannot see. We cannot see cosmic, gamma, or X-rays, ultraviolet light, infrared light, radar, or television, or radio waves to mention a few. There are also sounds that exist that we cannot hear, and many other unseen things we have not yet heard or discovered.

It reminds me of the time my brother-in-law took me out for my first snorkeling experience. He had told me how scuba diving and snorkeling allowed him to see the wonders of a coral reef and the beauty of different fish species. Now I was going to see it for myself as I followed him into the water.

We stood in the clear blue-green water about chest deep and he instructed me how to put on the snorkeling mask and use the breathing tube. However, when I tried breathing through the small air tube the trouble began as I could not suck in enough air and felt like I was drowning. I began gasping for air, which made me hyperventilate and my heart began to race. I jerked off the mask and tried to breathe deeply, while telling myself that this was crazy as I was in no danger of drowning. When my nerves calmed down I put the mask back on and tried to breath through the breathing tube and the same thing happened again. I had to try several times before I could breathe through the air tube without any issues.

As I leaned over and put my face into the water, making sure the air tube stayed above the water, I was astonished to see an aquarium with vegetation and the most beautiful fish I had ever seen. This was a new and exhilarating experience. It amazed me that I could not see or experience this sight while standing in the water. I held out my handful of frozen peas and the fish swam right up and ate them. Before long I was swimming all over the lake and seeing other fish and sights.

Later we took a break on the shore and I told him how I could not fully grasp all he had told me about the unseen world underneath the water. It amazed me that even though we were standing in the water I did not see anything until I put my face in the water.

Furthermore, I thanked him for being patient and helping me through the anxiety attacks I suffered from trying to breathe through the air tube, which almost robbed me of the most wonderful experience I had ever had in the water. Then I told him I wanted to share with him about an invisible world I had experienced and wanted him to experience.

I shared about my experience with Jesus and the invisible kingdom of God. Then I explained that if I had not trusted and followed him into the water I would not have enjoyed what he had experienced. In like manner if he would trust and follow me he could also have the same experience of seeing the invisible kingdom of God. In a few minutes he prayed with me and turned his life over to Jesus and the invisible kingdom of God became real to him.

It thrills me to see that with every improvement man makes in bridging the gap between the seen and unseen is the realization that there is an unseen world. These realities, however, have created a paradox in the scientific world, which only deals with the natural and physical realms, as there are no means for scientist to prove or disprove the spiritual realm. Therefore the only true source one can turn to for answers is the Bible. Keep in mind, however, that the Bible does not contain scientific books, but where it does address scientific subjects it has been proven over and over to be accurate.

We read in Hebrews 11: 6 (emphasis added) "But without faith it is impossible to please Him, *for he who comes to God must believe that He is, and that He is a rewarder of those who diligently seek Him.*" Here we learn that faith enables one to believe that God is. Therefore I define religion as mankind worshipping a god he either knows or thinks he knows. If his worship is not based upon Scriptures he is worshiping ideas about God and not God himself. The good news is that God has given faith to each of us (Romans 12:3). Thus anyone can know God exists.

I'm not sure who wrote the following illustration but it does make a valid point: A man went to a barbershop to have his haircut and his beard trimmed. As the barber began to work, they began to have a good conversation. They talked about many things and various subjects. When they eventually touched on the subject of God, the barber said, "I don't believe that God exists."

"Why do you say that?" asked the customer?

"Well, you just have to go out in the street to realize that God doesn't exist. Tell me, if God exists, would there be so many sick people? Would there be abandoned children? If God existed, there would be neither suffering nor pain. I can't imagine a loving God who would allow all of these things."

The customer thought for a moment, but didn't respond because he didn't want to start an argument. The barber finished his job, and the customer left the shop. Just after he left the barbershop, he saw a man in the street with long, stringy, dirty hair and an untrimmed beard. He looked dirty and unkempt. The customer turned back and entered the barbershop again, and he said to the barber, "You know what? Barbers do not exist."

"How can you say that?" asked the surprised barber. "I am here, and I am a barber. And I just worked on you!"

"No!" the customer exclaimed. "Barbers don't exist because if they did, there would be no people with dirty long hair and untrimmed beards, like that man outside."

"Ah, but barbers do exist! That's what happens when people do not come to me."

"Exactly!" affirmed the customer. "That's the point! God, too, does exist! That's what happens when people do not go to Him and don't look to Him for help. That's why there's so much pain and suffering in the world."

OK, so God exists but whom or what is He?

We are told in Genesis 1:1 "In the beginning God"... no details of how He began because He is self-existing and not created as seen in Revelation 1:8 "He is the Alpha and Omega, the Beginning and the Ending, who is and who was and who is to come, the Almighty."

Although the process of creation is unknown we know that anything that exists was caused to exist. So whatever caused the universe to come into existence must be greater than the universe. Thus the reality of our universe is proof that God exist just as light gives proof the sun exists and oxygen verifies the existence of air.

Believing God exists is one of the greatest miracles you can experience. Think comprehending the incomprehensible. Consider also that if God could be reduced to our understanding He would not be God. Somehow God is able to overcome all our questions, objections, and doubts about his existence and draw us unto himself. If we respond in a positive manner and have a spiritual encounter with Him he becomes real and we have the audacity to say we know He exists even though we do not know who He is or have never seen Him.

The Bible gives us four vital definitions of who God is:

> He is spirit and truth (John 4:24).
> He is love (1 John 4:8).
> He is light (1 John 1:5).
> He is fire (Hebrews 12:29).

There are also four vital Biblical attributes of God;

> He is Omnipotent (all-powerful) as seen in Psalms 62:11.
> He is Omnipresence (presence everywhere)—Proverbs 15:3.
> He is Omniscience (all knowing)—John 3:20.
> And He is creator of all things—Nehemiah 9:6.

The Godhead also has diversity with unity:

> The Father initiates (John 12:49).
> The Son mediates (1 Timothy 2:5).
> The Holy Spirit executes (John 14:26).

Because God is a spirit He is not subject to natural and physical laws because He created them. The laws that control Him are spiritual. We, on the other hand, are subject to all three laws—natural, physical, and spiritual.

Because mankind is created in the image of God we have the unique ability to think, reason, have ideas, be creative, choose and make decisions, but it does not make us God. Therefore you cannot compare God to people or any created thing and accept God to be whom He reveals Himself to be.

While the greatest miracle one can experience is to realize God exist, the next miracle is just as important—knowing God in all three dimensions. The first one we will study is knowing God as your father.

TWO

God Our Father

The first and vital dimension of God we need to wrap our minds around for spiritual growth is the revelation and understanding the father nature of God. There are those who have a hard time believing God as Father because concepts of God come mainly from the relationship with a natural father. Furthermore, if your father was not a godly man he could not reflect the true nature of fatherhood. And For those who never knew their natural father it becomes even more difficult to accept God as a loving, caring, and good Father.

I can attest to this truth with regard to not knowing your natural father. I was conceived in an adulterous relationship, and never knew my father. My mother had her affair as retaliation for her husband's womanizing lifestyle. Soon thereafter they were divorced and she married another Smith who was older, an alcoholic, and mean spirited. He was constantly getting drunk and threatening to kill us. I grew up with an older brother, whom Mr. Smith made leave our home when he was a teenager, and a sister. My mother's first husband is listed on my birth certificate as father. For some reason when I was in my twenty's I began to sense he was not my father. Just before my mother died I got up the nerve to ask her who my father was and she told me the story.

Mom finally divorced Mr. Smith and did the best she could to raise three children, at times working two jobs. We lived in the poorest area of Huntsville, Alabama and although we were poor Mom always made sure we had clean clothes to wear.

During this time I was full of fear and clung to Moms leg and hid behind her dress if others were present. When I entered the first grade the other children picked up on my insecurity and tormented me in various ways so I know how it fills to be bullied by other children.

Mom always took us to church so I grew up knowing about Jesus. In fact I liked to play church where I would be the preacher and the other children would be the congregation. But in my teen years I became very rebellious and got into a lot of trouble in school and with the law. I'll spare you boring details of my school years, where teachers passed me primarily because they did not want me back in their class. My older sister, on the other hand was an honor student and this enabled her to get a scholarship to attend college.

Because I could not get a job after graduating from high school I begrudgingly joined the army for two years. I hated the army with all its rules and regulations and was in constant trouble. So when my sister told me she could get me enrolled in college and I could get out of the army three months early I went for it even though I thought if I could not pass high school courses, how am I going to pass college-level courses?

I decide, therefore, to attend one term of college and then go live in California.

Once enrolled, however, I began to wonder if I put forth my best effort could I pass the courses? So I studied hard and to my surprise made excellent grades in all my classes. This success led me to stay in college and continue my education. I graduated with a B.S. degree in chemistry, but had a hard time finding a job due to the Depression in 1959. A consulting lab in St. Louis, finally hired me, and it was while living there I encountered Jesus and was born again.

In recalling my life journey, I remember that after I made the choice to acknowledge Jesus as my Lord and Savior, I got involved in a local church, and continued to be involved in church wherever we lived. Very quickly I was asked to teach a Sunday school class. No one considered my calling or qualification to teach, but based the request solely on a need for a teacher. I was told to use the teacher's guide to teach each Sunday's lesson as it explained the Scripture and how to discuss whatever subjects the lessons were about.

I did not realize at the time that I was under the bondage of rejection and trying to earn God's love through performance. I could never say, "No" when asked to serve in any capacity, even though I may not have wanted to or was not qualified for that service.

The curse of rejection is one of Satan's major weapons to keep one from knowing they are loved and accepted due to what Jesus did. For some, it makes them fearful God is out to get them and would never love and accept them.

The writers of books called the Old Testament only knew God according to the Law that taught "an eye for an eye, and a tooth for a tooth." However they spoke of God being the Father. Isaiah, for example wrote, "Doubtless You are our Father, Though Abraham was ignorant of us, and Israel does not acknowledge us. You, O LORD, are our Father; Our Redeemer from Everlasting is Your name" (Isaiah 63:16). And David wrote in Psalms 68:5, "A father of the fatherless, a defender of widows, is God in His holy habitation."

It is only when Jesus comes upon the earth and presents God as Father that we see the contrast of the harshness of the Law and the nature of Father God. Thus we find that in religion he is God and in relationships he is Father.

Notice Jesus showing the tenderness of God in Matthew 6:8-9, ". . . for your Father knows what things you have need of before you ask him. Pray, then in this way: Our Father . . . ." Here we find God is our Father and is personally aware of our needs. Furthermore we see he is caring and not harsh and impersonal.

Jesus also spoke of God as his father in John 14:23, "Jesus answered and said to him, "'If anyone loves Me, he will keep My word; and *My Father* will love him, and We will come to him and make Our home with him.'" (Emphasis mine.) This reveals the intimate and personal nature of our Father which is also found in John 3:16, "For God so loved the world that he gave his only begotten Son."

The Apostle Paul also takes God out of the hard, harsh, and impersonal religious environment into a personal relationship as Father to his children in Ephesians 3:14-15, "For this reason I bow my knees unto the Father of our Lord Jesus Christ, of whom the whole family in heaven and earth is named."

Scriptures reveal God as our father as seen in Psalms 139:13-18, "For You formed my inward parts; You covered me in my mother's womb. I will praise You, for I am fearfully and wonderfully made; Marvelous are Your works, And that my soul knows very well. My frame was not hidden from You, when I was made in secret, And skillfully wrought in the lowest parts of the earth. Your eyes saw my substance, being yet unformed. And in Your book they all were written, the days fashioned for me, when as yet there were none of them." God forming us in our mother's womb makes God our Father.

The Prophet Jeremiah confirms this truth in Jeremiah 1:4-5, "Then the word of the LORD came to me, saying: ""Before I formed you in the womb I knew you; before you were born I sanctified you; I ordained you a prophet to the nations.'"

The common themes I want you to see from these Scriptures is that we are a product of God's love. God was thinking of us and laid out our days and his plans for us before time began. Therefore, God's purpose for our life began before conception and not after we were born.

So, who is your daddy—God, who is your mother—God? Your natural father and mother are the ones God chose to be his instruments to give you a natural birth. If you can wrap your mind around this truth it will free you of the deception that your parents, good, bad or whatever, determines who you are and your purpose or lot in life.

Jesus emphatically states that He desires for us to go beyond the revelation of Him as our Lord and Savior and be drawn to the Father as revealed in John 14:6, "Jesus said unto him, I am the way, the truth, and the life: No man comes unto the Father, but by me." When Philip heard this he made a response that is in the heart of all mankind: "Lord, show us the Father."

I have been shown the father in so many ways since that day when He asked me to let Him be my ideal dad. In fact I wrote a chapter, "The Importance Of Fathers" in our book, "*The Joy Of Success In the Home*," to teach the truth that fathers represent God in the home.

Here are a few valuable truths Jesus revealed about our Father:

OUR FATHER IS A PROVIDER

In Luke 12: 22-32 Jesus addresses the problem of being anxious over our life—what we eat, wear and drink. He points out that God takes care of the birds and clothes the lilies with a beauty that even Solomon with all his riches could not obtain. He assures us that our Father knows our need of these things, and then gives us this revelation: "It is the Father's good pleasure to give you the kingdom."

Here we see our Father is a provider and liberal in his giving. He gives materially to his family, not as a substitute for his love, but as a demonstration of his love. He is aware of the needs of his family and will not withhold any good thing from them, and takes great pleasure in being able to meet their needs.

Our Father, furthermore, never uses blessings as a means to manipulate or control us. In fact, we find the Holy Spirit revealing in 2 Corinthians 5:14

that it is the love of Christ that restrains us. This is the relationship our father has with his children and desire we have with ours. A godly father desires that his children obey him and make correct choices out of love and trust, not out of fear of punishment or hope of reward.

THE FATHERS USE OF AUTHORITY

Jesus reveals how the Father exercised authority in John 5:19-20, "Jesus therefore answered them, the Son can do nothing of Himself, unless it is something He sees the Father doing; for whatever the Father does, these things the Son also does in like manner. For the Father loves the Son, and shows Him all things that He himself is doing and greater works than these will He show Him that you may marvel." Here we learn the Father was an example to Jesus in exercising authority and direction for his life. Jesus was convinced the Father loved Him because the Father took time to teach and train Him, and He wanted to be like and do the things His Father did.

This truth was demonstrated to me one time when a family asked us to joint them for a weekend in their condo on the beach. We arrived in the evening and sat in a cool breeze to see a beautiful sunset over the calm deep blue sea.

The following morning I noticed their young son opened the door and looked at us and then went back into his room. A few moments later he came out and joined us. I commented that he now had on the same color shorts and shirt and was wearing a watch just like his father. They told me that every morning he always checked to see what his dad was wearing and then dressed to look like him. It made me think of the old sayings, "like father like son", and "the apple never falls far from the tree."

THE FATHER AS A DISCIPLINARIAN

Jesus speaking to the lukewarm church of the Laodiceans said in Revelation 3: 19 "As many as I love, I rebuke and chasten." The word chasten implies 'instruction' and 'discipline' means to correct by punishment for the purpose of reclaiming. Notice our Father does this because he loves us. And in Hebrews chapter 11 we are told he does this that we may share in His holiness and obtain the peaceful fruit of righteousness.

A godly father has the good of his children in mind as he is thinking of how he can be a good steward of God's assignment in preparing them to fulfill God's purposes for their lives. In order to be successful the father must seek the best way to train and correct the child. Keep in mind that the purpose is to teach them they have freedom of choice but not freedom of consequences. It does not automatically mean spanking when they mess up. It may mean having to sit still until their attitude changes. It may mean not playing with a toy they were unwilling to share. It may be going hungry as a result of refusing to eat. And it may require more serious consequences depending upon the action and attitude of the child.

The child may not always understand that discipline is for his or her good nor will it always be a joyful experience for either party, but discipline should always be done in love for the good of the child.

THE FATHER IS SENSITIVE AND CARING

I stated earlier that Jesus showed us our Father knows our needs before we pray and desires to meet our needs. One important way to know the needs of your children is to develop the habit when they are babies to spend time praying over them at bedtime. When they are old enough to talk and express their thoughts lay down beside your child, as he begins to settle down he will open up his heart to you. As you talk and listen he will share with you anything that is troubling him or those things, about which he is worried. In so doing you are teaching your children to be intimate with their heavenly Father.

When he or she gets older and you no longer lay down with them, there is still the need to spend personal time where the two of you can talk. If you develop good communications with your children as babies you will discover that in their teen years they will seek your wisdom and counsel and not that of their peers or others.

Perhaps this is why God instructed fathers in Deuteronomy 6:7 to be diligent in teaching and training his children when he sits at home, when he walks by the way, when he lies down, and when he rises up. This requires the father to spend a lot of time with his children. Out of this natural relationship will come opportunities to mold and shape their lives for the purposes of God and being successful adults.

Notice how important it is to God that a man understands and obeys the call of fatherhood from Genesis 18:19, "For I know him, that he will command his children and his household after him, and they shall keep the way of the LORD, to do justice and judgment; that the Lord may bring upon Abraham that which he has spoken of him."

Abraham was 100 years old man when He became a father. Here is the good news, if a 100 year old man can learn to be a father so can we. I want to encourage you fathers to set your hearts to be a father like our heavenly father. I want to encourage you yet to be fathers to get a vision for being a father. And I want to encourage those who may have some hurts and fear about marriage or having children that God will enable you to have a heavenly home and children. It does not have to be like most of the homes where Jesus is not the head, and where the man does not show the father heart of God to his family. Abraham is proof of this reality.

THREE

Angels, Satan, and Demons

Here is a vital truth you must never forget as you go through your Christian life. In the invisible spiritual realm there are spiritual beings called angels some good and some evil. The existence and order of angelic beings can only be discovered from the Scriptures. Therefore I want to examine what some Scriptures reveal on this subject.

The prophets Ezekiel and Isaiah write revealing discourses with regard to Satan; in Ezekiel 28:12-15 the prophet reveals there is a spirit, who was in the Garden of Eden, "Full of wisdom and perfect in beauty," behind the power of Tyre, an ancient Phoenician city with a long and illustrious history. The commerce of the whole world was gathered into the warehouses of Tyre that consisted of two distinct parts, a rocky fortress on the mainland, called "Old Tyre," This city was built on a small, rocky island about half-a-mile distant from the shore. Whenever superior forces attacked the mainland they would retreat to the rocky island for safety, as the army could not cross over the water.

Shalmaneser, who was assisted by the Phoenicians of the mainland, besieged Tyre for five years, and Nebuchadnezzar (B.C. 586) for thirteen years without success, the result was a deception Tyre could never be defeated.

Then along came Alexander the Great. When they abandoned the mainland he demolished the city and pushed the rubble into the sea and made a road to the island. Then he rolled up a new weapon of war that could hurl stones and fire balls over the wall. After a siege of seven months they were defeated and Alexander tore down the city and it eventually became a place for fishermen to spread out their nets to dry, just as God had spoken through the prophet (Ezekiel. 26:2-5).

Isaiah 14:12-14 also speaks of Lucifer, who weakens the nations falling from heaven. From his description we learn Satan is a created being called the anointed cherub who covers, who is wise, beautiful, and musical. All was perfect until iniquity, the power to do evil, began to work; "For you have said in your heart: 'I will ascend into heaven, I will exalt my throne above the stars of God; I will also sit on the mount of the congregation on the farthest sides of the north; I will ascend above the heights of the clouds, I will be like the Most High."

In Revelation 12:9-10 we learn this thinking led to Satan deciding to overthrow the government of God. He persuaded other angels to join in his rebellion, which resulted in a war in heaven. When God's angel Michael and his angels won the war and "the great dragon was cast out, that serpent of old, called the Devil and Satan, who deceives the whole world; he was cast to the earth, and his angels were cast out with him." Then I heard a loud voice saying in heaven, "Now salvation, and strength, and the kingdom of our God, and the power of His Christ have come, for the accuser of our brethren, who accused them before our God day and night, has been cast down . . . ." Later in verse 12 we read, "Woe to the inhabitants of the earth and the sea! For the devil has come down to you, having great wrath, because he knows that he has a short time."

The names of Satan used in Scripture gives us an insight into his nature and personality that explains why the angels said, "woe to the inhabitants of the earth and the sea."

A. He is called "serpent, devil, dragon, deceiver, and accuser (Revelation 12:9, 10).

B. Adversary (I Peter 5:8).

C. Prince of demons (Matthew 12:24).

D. Evil one (Matthew 13:19).

E. Murderer and Liar (John 8:44).

F. Ruler of darkness (Ephesians 6:12).

G. Prince of this world (John 14:30).

H. Prince of the power of the air (Ephesians 2:2).

I. God of this world (II Corinthians 4:4).

J. He is called the tempt (Matthew 4:3).

K. An unclean spirit (Mark 12:43).

L. He is called the ruler of darkness (Ephesians 6:1).

These names of Satan reveal how evil he is and explains why Peter said we must always be on guard because our adversary goes about as a roaring lion seeking whom he may devour (1 Peter 5:8-9).

In my early years, I said in a very flippant way many times that Jesus had pulled all of the devil's teeth, and all he can do is roar. Then God showed me that even Michael, the great angel who knew Satan was a powerful angelic dignitary would not rail against him and said "The Lord rebuke you" (Jude 9).

People speak about Satan in a flippant manner, because they have no understanding of who he is. If you ever think he's just a toothless little old thing out there who can only roar and can't devour you it will deceive you into not being on guard. If he couldn't devour you, God would not tell you to be diligent; God would not tell you to be on your guard. Thus there are many men and women, including myself, who have already found out to their sorrow Satan can and will devour you if you do not stay on guard.

The book of Job reveals that although Job was righteous the devil accused him of fearing God only because he was being protected and blessed by God.

If God took away the protection and touched what he had then he would curse God to His face (Job 1:6-11).

As a born again believer under the lordship of Jesus and covered by His blood, the devil has no power over you until you in some way give him a legal basis to curse you. Therefore the devil is always finding ways to lure you away from the covering and safety of God.

The primary weapon used to draw us away is found in 1Timothy 4:1-6, "Now the Spirit expressly says that in latter times some will depart from the faith, giving heed to seducing spirits and doctrines of demons, speaking lies in hypocrisy, having their own conscience seared with a hot iron, forbidding to marry, and commanding to abstain from foods which God created to be received with thanksgiving by those who believe and know the truth. For every creature of God is good, and nothing to be refused, if it be received with thanksgiving for it is sanctified by the word of God and prayer. If you instruct the brethren in these things, you will be a good minister of Jesus Christ, nourished in the words of faith and of the good doctrine, which you have carefully followed." The Apostle Paul tells us it is listening to seducing spirits and doctrine of demons that causes some to depart from the faith.

To get us on the same page I am going to define some words found in this passage;

- Heed means to turn the mind to, attend to, be attentive, to apply one's self to, to attach one's self to, hold or cleave to a person or a thing.
- To seduce is to cause to roam from truth, virtue, and safety. It is to persuade one into disobedience or disloyalty. It is to lead or draw one into an evil or foolish or disastrous course. It means to entice, to tempt, and to corrupt. In some versions it reads deceiving spirits.
- To deceive means to mislead, cheat, to deal falsely, to be untrue in word or deed.

- Doctrine means that which is taught as principles of faith, theology, and philosophy. Notice the way seducing or deceiving spirits operate is called doctrine of demons.

Let me be very clear on this truth; there are only two types of doctrines—the doctrine of Jesus and the doctrine of demons. The doctrine of Jesus will always be according to godliness and the doctrine of demons will always be contrary to Jesus teachings (1 Timothy 6:3)

Here we are told there are seducing spirits in the invisible world. Notice spirit is plural, so there are more than one spirit and ways you can be seduced. For any who may have been deceived that demon and other spirits do not exist there are other Scripture that speak of spirits such as 2 Timothy 1:7 "God has not given us a spirit of fear". So fear is a spirit.

The Apostle John also addresses deceivers in 2 John 7-11, "For many deceivers have gone out into the world who does not confess Jesus Christ as coming in the flesh. This is a deceiver and an antichrist. Look to yourselves, that we do not lose those things we worked for, but that we may receive a full reward. Whoever transgresses and does not abide in the doctrine of Christ does not have God. He who abides in the doctrine of Christ has both the Father and the Son. If anyone comes to you and does not bring this doctrine, do not receive him into your house nor greet him; for he who greets him shares in his evil deeds."

I remember someone wrote a book about 88 reasons Jesus was going to return in 1988. I had several people call and ask if I had read the book and what I thought about it. My response was that I did not waste my time reading the book, as I knew it was a doctrine of demons because Jesus said no one but the Father knows when He will return. Then there were billboards that advertise the world is ending on May 21st that upset a lot of people.

I also received e-mail about a Time magazine cover, "What If There Is No Hell," referring to Rob Bell's book *Love Wins*. I have not read the book nor will I because I know this is a demonic doctrine to seduce one into thinking there is no hell. However it is a thought-provoking question—how many churchgoers would stop attending church and serving in the church if they were convinced that there was no hell.

I raise this question because seducing spirits and doctrine of demons teach two dangerous lies. If you believe in God, and said a prayer you are a Christian and can now live without fear of going to hell. The second is that you can have one foot in the kingdom of God and another in the world.

Lets examine this in light of what Jesus teaches in 2 Timothy 3:1-5, "But know this, that in the last days perilous times will come: For men will be lovers of themselves, lovers of money, boasters, proud, blasphemers, disobedient to parents, unthankful, unholy, unloving, unforgiving, slanderers, without self-control, brutal, despisers of good, traitors, headstrong, haughty, lovers of pleasure rather than lovers of God, having a form of godliness but denying its power. And from such people turn away!"

Here we learn the doctrine "just believe" can have a form of godliness. One can learn how to be religious, to sing, to raise their hands, to say the right words. But if it is only a form the person is deceived.

Let me challenge your thinking in a way that may stir up religious demons; to say all one has to do to be saved is believe is a doctrine of demons. In fact we are told that demons believe in God and they are not going to be in heaven. (James 2:9).

Let me take this a further step, if the gospel we preach that Jesus saves does not change you from living to please self to pleasing God, or to reckon yourself dead to sin and alive unto God, then this gospel cannot get you to heaven because the wages of sin is death not heaven. In fact the only way you can be absolutely sure you are truly born again is that sin now bothers you.

Another very dangerous doctrine, straight from the pit of hell, is that you do not have to come out and be separate from the world. God commands us to come out and be separated from the world in 2 Corinthians 6:17-18, "Therefore, Come out from among them and be separate," says the Lord. "Do not touch what is unclean, and I will receive you." I will be a Father to you, and you shall be My sons and daughters, says the LORD Almighty."

A 6th century Chinese general, Sun Tza, wrote a book, "The Art Of War," that has been the guide for military thinking for centuries and a variety of others such as leadership, politics and sports. He wrote, "All warfare is based on deception. Hence when able to attack we must seem unable; when using our forces, we must seem inactive; when we are near, we must make the enemy believe we are far away; when far away, we must make him believe we are near." Likewise the enemy of our souls, Satan, wages war against us based on deceit; just he did Adam and Eve.

Jesus tells the Jews who were trying to kill him why they were doing this in John 8:44, "You are of your father the devil, and the desires of your father you want to do. He was a murderer from the beginning, and does not stand in the truth, because there is no truth in him. When he speaks a lie, he speaks from his own resources, for he is a liar and the father of it.

I want to read this from The Message; "You're from your father, the Devil, and all you want to do is please him. He was a killer from the very start. He couldn't stand the truth because there wasn't a shred of truth in him. When the Liar speaks, he makes it up out of his lying nature and fills the world with lies." Here is a truth you need to write down; behind every sin is a lie.

All behavior is based on belief and our belief system is conclusions we have made about ourselves, about God, about others, and about life. If these belief's are wrong our thinking becomes a snare because as one thinks so is he. Therefore, you can be very sincere and be sincerely wrong.

For the sake of time I am only going to look at three areas of false beliefs about self that are very deceptive;

1. *I have the power to control my life.* This belief is called humanism and is the result of our wanting to be god. It was this desire to be god that Satan used to seduce Adam and Eve into believing they could eat fruit from the tree of knowledge of good and evil and they would be like God. Here we have the first doctrine of demons, God said eating this fruit would result in death, Satan said it would not.

The belief that I possess the power to conquer the problems I create is supported by almost everything we read—except the Bible. This power theology plays havoc in our lives. Sometimes we almost kill ourselves trying to demonstrate how powerful we are. In sports it's called competition.

Believing I have the power to control my life and need to do so is rooted in our self-worth. We read that the world is full of lies. The world's system of worth is based upon a false value system. The world has established worth is determined by such things as money, fame, houses, sports, cars, positions of authority, beauty, athletic ability, musical ability, intellect, professional achievements, race, and others opinions that are based on artificial performance.

However in the Kingdom of God we find that each of us are so valuable we were worth God sending his Son Jesus to die on a cross to redeem and free us from the bondages of a sin cursed world.

These deceptive beliefs the world has created results in all types of stress. Fear of failure is a horrible bondage. It declares that we are not as powerful as we thought. When others are able to preform better than us we will be resentful, because it implies that they are more god-like than we are. Those who are trapped in this deception freak out when they fail to meet others expectation and their emotions produce various reactions. They may respond with anger, resentment, worry, anxiety, depression, jealousy, strife, envy, etc. Furthermore we may withdraw, become hostile, argue, be rude, and defame the character of others, etc.

On the other hand, those who turn the control of their life over to Jesus find they are loved and accepted. Being secure in God's love will set you free from the deception you must be in control of your life.

2. **I am right and have truth** is another deception of Self. We are convinced through our belief system that we are right in our understanding of truth. The world tells us that if it we think something is right it is right for us as truth is relative and not absolute.

I remember riding to work one day with an engineer who was upset over a U.S. Senator having sex with a page who worked for him. Knowing he did not believe in the existence of God I saw this as an opportunity to challenge his philosophy and asked him, "What's wrong with that?"

He seemed shocked at my question and said, "What do you mean what's wrong with that?"

I replied, "If the senator thinks its okay then what's the problem?" This really set him off and he proceeded to tell me how it was morally wrong for the senator to take advantage of a young page who worked for him. When he finished I asked him where his idea that something is right or wrong came from. He almost yelled at me when he said, "I know what you're trying to do. You want me to say"—God—", and I'm not going to do it."

If we ever stop to listen to the conversations in restaurants, bars, or wherever people gather we would hear them trying to establish their worth by bragging about their possessions, where they have been and what they have done or whatever they believe will exalt them above others.

Think of all the arguments over small points of trivia. Someone gets into an argument over the meaning of a word and to prove who is right they look up the word in a dictionary. The looser then responds, "Well it's not the unabridged Oxford dictionary that has more definitions than this one."

It all has to do with the desire to be god-like. We do not want to be equal or under others, we want to be over, superior and more god-like than them.

3. *I should be loved and accepted by everyone.* The truth is that some people will take one look at you and decide they do not even like you. The more you try to earn their love and acceptance the more they reject and do things to hurt you. The more this happens the more insecure you

become and wonder what is wrong with you. To avoid this deception realize life is not always fair and move on with your life.

I have hit this doctrine of salvation hard because I know that once the issue is settled in your heart and mind that Jesus is your Lord and that his word is the final authority for your life, the Holy Spirit will lead you into the abundant life that Jesus promised. If you are teachable and under the Lordship of Jesus, when you get off track, the Holy Spirit will get you back on the right pathway because the right attitude of the heart will always keep you going in the right direction.

Now let's move on to just what it means to be saved because there are so many sincere God loving people who do not know who they are in Jesus or this truth has not been presented in such a way they believe it.

For example, many traditional religious hymns put off complete redemption until after we die. They teach we are going to rest when we get to heaven; we are going to have victory when we get to heaven, we are going to be over comers when we get to heaven, but while on earth we are to expect failure, weakness, sickness, disease, misery, and disappointments.

Scripture, however, teaches that if you are in Christ you are a new creature and old things have passed away (2 Corinthians 5:17-21). What old things was the Apostle Paul talking about? He was speaking with regards to salvation by the law. He preached that Jesus was the new way God had provided for all to be saved. In this new way God had done something through Jesus the law could not do in providing a way for us be reconciled to God. It involves a new way of thinking, a new way of believing and a new way of relating to God.

In fact, through Jesus we become a new creation and something that never before existed. So just what is it that we have become? Here are a few to consider:

a. The dwelling place of God (2 Corinthians 6:16).
b. A son of God (John 1:12).

c.   The temple of the Holy Spirit (1 Corinthians 6:19).

d.   A lively stone being built into the house of God (1 Peter 2:5).

We also learn from this passage that Jesus who knew no sin became sin for us in order that we could be righteous. To be righteous is to be just, correct and lawful, which can only be ascribed to one person—God. Now I want you to see and understand what is being said. Scripture does not say we are made righteous but that we become the righteousness of God. This is the greatest revelation the Holy Spirit can impart to you about salvation. It defies all human reasoning and nullifies all weapons of the Devil. Let me show you why this is true.

Most of us will have no trouble agreeing with the first part of what Jesus did—became sin for us but what about the second part? Did you become the righteousness of God when you got saved or do you become righteous after death or is it simply reckoned to us and we never actually become righteous? If I am the righteousness of God, in Jesus his anointed one, just how righteous am I?

Let's look at some more new truths. We read in Romans 5:1, "Therefore, having been justified by faith; we have peace with God through our Lord Jesus Christ." What does it mean to be justified? When are we justified and have this peace with God? Is it true I am no longer a sinner and the righteousness of God has cleared me of my debt? Can I have peace now or must I wait until after death and hopefully get to heaven?

Let's add to this from Romans 8: 31-34, "What shall we then say to these things? If God *be* for us, who *can be* against us? He that spared not his own Son, but delivered him up for us all, how shall he not with him also freely give us all things? Who shall lay any thing to the charge of God's elect? *It is* God that justifies. Who *is* he that condemned? *It is* Christ that died, yea rather, that is risen again, who is even at the right hand of God, who also makes intercession for us."

We read, "Who shall lay anything to the charge of God's elect?" The elect of God are those chosen in Christ before the foundation of the world, unto eternal life and salvation. But are those who are so blessed free from the penalty of Adam's sin? If true, and they are cleared of the multitudes of sins, some of them very great ones, and are now righteous is there anyone who will rise up with charges they are not righteous?

Yes, there is one, Satan, the accuser of the brethren, lays many things to our charge, and so do the men of the world; but all these charges avail nothing, because none of the divine persons, Father, Son, and Spirit, lay anything against us because God the Father, has justified Christians from every charge and pronounced them righteous.

The truth is that Christians are now the righteousness of God and cleared of all charges we are told in Romans 8:1, (emphasis added) *"There is therefore no condemnation to them who are in Jesus."* If I know I am righteous, justified, and cleared of my sin debt then I will not be under condemnation.

Furthermore, we find in Colossians 2:10, "and you are complete in Him, who is the head of all principality and power." When are we complete? Is it now or in the life to come? If I am not complete what has God left undone in His redemption? Did he just provide for some forgiveness or all? If you think life after death is to cleanse you from sin and provide all the blessings of redemption you are faced with the dilemma that God was unable to give you complete victory and needs the Devil to complete his redemptive work. Remember death is the result of sin and only deals with our physical body not our spirit or soul. The truth is that God has done a complete work—it is finished.

The understanding of our righteousness is essential in winning as we journey through life as revealed in Romans 5:17, "For if by the one man's offense death reigned through the one, much more those who receive abundance of grace and of the gift of righteousness will reign in life through the One, Jesus Christ." We do not grow in righteousness, as you are as righteous now as you will ever be. You are as saved now, as you will ever be. You are as forgiven now, as you will will ever be.

Here is another awesome truth in Romans 8:37, "Nay, in all these things we are more than conquerors through him that loved us." When are we to be more than conquers? Is it in this life or in the next one? Is it possible to live in victory now over all power of the Devil and sin or must we wait until we get to heaven? Many sincere Christians feel unworthy because they still sin, and have weaknesses or whatever that deceived them into doubting the truth of God's word that they are righteous and can now live a victorious life.

But Brother Joe you don't know me. I struggle in this area. I sin in this area. I compromise in this area. I act ungodly in this way. Will it surprise you when I tell you God is aware of how you live and act? I am of the opinion the problem is due to not understanding the difference between God *imputing* righteousness to us and *imparting* righteousness to us. When we repent of not acknowledging God as our Lord and make the decision to no longer live to please self but live to please Him we are born again and become a new creature—a son of God and God imputes His righteousness to us.

Let me illustrate; When God looks down from heaven at a Christian He sees him covered over with Jesus robe of righteousness. However when we look at ourselves we see from underneath the robe and look at the flesh and can see weakness or sin and come under condemnation. Keep in mind condemnation is not of God. The Holy Spirit will convict you and challenge you to repent but He will not condemn you. With God there is always hope and encouragement. There is always love, compassion and forgiveness. Remember, God allows you to see the falling short of His glory to remind you that you are still an earthen vessel and need Him to impart His righteousness to you. When you repent this allows the impartation of His righteousness and you become more like Jesus.

I know this may be hard to believe due to being told all our lives in one way or another that we have to prove by our performance we deserve to be loved and accepted. Many sincere God loving Christians wrongly believe you must in some way earn forgiveness and righteousness.

There is a person in the Bible who causes serious problems with this concept—Dismus. You may not have heard of him. I only recently heard this name. On the day Jesus died three crosses were raised. Jesus hung on the center one between two criminals. One of the men mocked Jesus, but the other said to Him, "Remember me when you come into Your kingdom." Jesus responded," Today you shall be with me in paradise." Historians tell us Dismus was this criminal. Although Dismus did not say the "sinners prayer", was never water baptized, or do any works, or performed in any way, Jesus granted his request, Dismus, therefore refutes the wrong theology of God's grace and forgiveness being based on performance and works rather than the righteousness of God.

If a child is kidnapped and the parents appeared on TV with the attitude of we love our child and we're sorry he has been kidnapped but hey, he should have known better as I told him many times to stay away from strangers. There is no right-minded person who would agree with them. In fact it would cause great concern as to how they could be so callous and unloving.

Suppose the child stays home and grows up as a wonderful child and then commits a terrible crime. The parents are shocked and disappointed but they do not stop loving the child. They show up at the jail, if possible they bail him out, and hire a lawyer. They stand by him and hope for the best.

In like manner we are told in Romans Chapter 3 that God had a right to redeem us from the power and dominion of Satan and sin because He is our Father. If we will accept what Jesus has done our repentance will allow God to impute His righteousness to us, clear us of all charges of sin, and make us whole and complete.

Then He can begin the process of setting us free from the root of all our troubles, which is self-love that is expressed as I must look good, feel good, be right, be in control, have power, money and live the "good" life so I can be happy.

As a Christian it may not be so much about getting, as I must prove I am worthy of God's love and acceptance. I must show by my performance of reading the Bible, prayer, going to church meetings, serving, and whatever shows that I really am saved and God will bless me. Being convinced you are now righteous will deliver you from the deception that you must earn God's love and forgiveness. It will also empower you to rule and reign enjoying a truly happy lifestyle.

Here is the good news. God is committed to conforming us into the image of Jesus and He has staying power. He is faithful and will complete the work He has started. He will bring us to the place where it is no longer I who lives but it is Christ in me the hope of glory.

There are many books on the subject of angels so I will just mention a few essential truths: We are told in Hebrews 1:13-14 that good angels are called ministering spirits for those who will inherit salvation. Further, we learn from Daniel 7:10 and Matthew 26:53 that they are very numerous. These good angels rejoice over a penitent sinner, Luke 15:10, bear the souls of the redeemed to paradise, Luke 16:22, and will be the harvesters at the end of this age (Matthew 13:39-41). On the other hand, the angels who joined Satan are called fallen angels; evil angels, demons, and they are destined to spend eternity in hell (Jude 6; Psalms 78:49; 2 Peter 2:4). An interesting side note is that hell was prepared for these angels, and has been enlarged to also receive fallen mankind (Matthew 25:41; Isaiah 5:14).

There is no Biblical record of angelic appearances to man till after the call of Abraham. From that time onward there are frequent references to their ministry on earth. They appear to rebuke idolatry in Judges 2:1-4 to call Gideon in Judges 6:11-12 and to consecrate Samson in Judges

13:3. In the days of the prophets, from Samuel onward, the angels appear only on behalf of the prophets.

The Incarnation of Jesus introduced a new era in the ministrations of angels. The gospel accounts reveal angels declared his birth, resurrection, and ascension and ministered to him after his temptation and agony.

Angels are shown to possess superhuman intelligence and power and to function primarily as agents of God's providence in carrying on his great work of redemption, as seen in Psalms 103:20-21, "Bless the LORD, you His angels, who excel in strength, who do His word, heeding the voice of His word. Bless the LORD, all *you* His hosts, *you* ministers of His, who do His pleasure."

Angels were not created in the image of God and are not to be worshipped. Humans were created in His image and are not like angels, and they also are not be worshipped. However we are told that in heaven we will be like unto the angels.

Let me remind you the devil is not God, but he can seduce you with false teachings to depart from the faith, as we shall see in the next chapter.

FOUR

Satan and the First Man – Adam

Scriptures reveal there are invisible beings called angels. One was named Satan who began thinking he could govern creation better than God. He convinced other angels to join in an attempt to overthrow the government of God and establish him as ruler of heaven. This resulted in a war in heaven and the defeat of Satan and his angels. The defeated angels were then banished from heaven and cast down to earth (Revelation 12).

Flip Wilson, a comedian who use to have a TV show, would do something wrong and say, "The devil made me do it." He may have been more right than wrong. But because he did it in a very humorous way the net effect was to insinuate Satan did not exist.

The Bible does not give us detailed information about devils until Jesus begins his ministry. Devils in the New Testament are spoken of as spiritual beings; they belong to the number of those angels that "kept not their first estate, "and are "unclean spirits." (Jude 1:6; Matthew 10:1). They are shown to believe God is and to be at enmity with Him, and recognizing Jesus as the Son of God (James 2:19; Matthew 8:29). In Ephesians 6:12 they are the "principalities and powers" against which we must "wrestle"

It is Satan and fallen angels' character that makes them devils. They kill, destroy, war, and spread sickness and disease. They also corrupt the elements of nature to carry out their works such as wind, fire, floods, draught, and earthquakes.

Furthermore, Satan and his angels are not restrained by sentiments, which soften and move human hearts. He has a great intellect that is driven and inspired by a corrupt, evil, cruel and vicious nature that has no pity or sympathy. He is fierce and resolute in seeking whom he may devour and does not limit his activities to one individual. Thus we find he deceives nations and influences governments to act for him. Even in our nation we can point to many examples of this truth such as the unconstitutional separation of church and state, laws to permit abortion, laws that disallow prayer in school, restrict religious activities, but support diversity, tolerance, homosexuality, same sex marriage, and persecution of Christianity.

We can also see the work Satan has done in the church. A few examples are ordination of homosexual as Bishop in the Episcopal and Lutheran Churches, ministers in the Methodist church, and pedophiles in the Catholic Priesthood. There are also "ministers" who support same sex marriages and abortion.

Perhaps his most devastating work is substituting the gain of worldly material as a sign of God's anointing, blessings, and true spiritual growth. The strength of the church lies in its devotion to God, not by how large it is, or how much money it takes in every week. A church that is devoted to God will usher in the presence and power of God and it is the presence of God that changes everything. Furthermore it is the prayers and power of the Holy Spirit that determines the strength of a church and gives it the ability to extend the kingdom of God.

When Satan and his angels were cast out of heaven a voice from heaven said, "woe to the earth and sea, because the devil has come down to you, having great wrath, knowing that he has only a short time " (Revelation 12:12). It is in the book of Genesis that we get our first glimpse as to why the angels said woe to you on Earth.

God placed the first man on earth—Adam, in the Garden of Eden and commanded him to rule, reign and take dominion over the earth and all living things. There were two special trees in the Garden, the tree of life, and the tree of knowledge of good and evil. God commanded Adam to not eat fruit from the tree of the knowledge of good and evil and that if he did he would die (Genesis 1-2).

To die means to make powerless, to separate, to make inoperative and to render ineffective. Thus when our spirit and soul separates from our body we call this death, as the body is made inoperative. When sin enters our life we are separated from God and made spiritually powerless. This is called spiritual death. If one dies physically without being born again he will remain eternally separated from God and this is called the second death.

There came a time when God created a wife for Adam from his rib and she was named Eve. At first all was well but in the course of time Satan came to the Garden and used a serpent to talk to Eve as seen in Genesis 3:1-13, "Now the serpent was more cunning than any beast of the field, which the Lord God had made. And he said to the woman, "Has God indeed said, 'You shall not eat of every tree of the garden'? "And the woman said to the serpent, "'we may eat the fruit of the trees of the garden; "but of the fruit of the tree which is in the midst of the garden, God has said, 'You shall not eat it, nor shall you touch it, lest you die.'" Then the serpent said to the woman, "'You will not surely die. "For God knows that in the day you eat of it your eyes will be opened, and you will be like God, knowing good and evil'"

Satan's deceptive powers and subtle means of accusing God are revealed in this conversation. He appears to be congratulatory and happy for Adam and Eve to be in the garden. Then he raises a question with regard to eating of the fruit on the trees. When Eve explains they were not to touch or eat fruit from the tree of knowledge of good and evil, Satan claimed it was because God did not want them to be God. Then he called God a liar by saying they would not die if they ate the forbidden fruit.

We are told in Genesis 3:6, "And when the woman saw that the tree *was* good for food, and that it *was* pleasant to the eyes, and a tree to be desired to make *one* wise, she took of the fruit thereof, and did eat, and gave also unto her husband with her; and he did eat." We find in I Timothy 2:14 that Eve was deceived into eating the forbidden fruit and Adam willfully disobeyed.

From their encounter with Satan we learn the importance of our eyes and ears, and the danger in trying to reason with him. Their first fatal mistake was listening and we saw earlier that giving heed to seducing spirits and doctrine of demons cause some to depart from the faith. This is why we are told over and over in Scripture to be careful how and what we hear.

Eve saw the tree was pleasant and this created a desire in her emotions. Once the emotions became involved and Eve reacted to what she saw and heard she was seduced and deceived to eat the forbidden fruit. This is why I teach that emotions do not think or reason but only react to what we see and hear. Because emotions are reaction we must guard our hearts and mind as our thoughts can put our emotions in charge and God did not create us to be emotionally controlled but spirit controlled.

After Adam and Eve had disobeyed God came to the Garden and asked Adam a simple yet penetrating question: "Where are you" (Genesis 3:9)? Adam replies that he was hiding due to being fearful and ashamed. Obviously something has changed for in the past Adam had freely walked and talked with God, but now he is hiding. God did not ask this question because He did not know where Adam was but to see if Adam was willing to take responsibility for his disobedience.

God's follow up question was more convicting than the first: "Have you eaten from the tree which I commanded you that you should not eat" (Genesis 3:11)? Rather than take personal responsibility for his sin Adam starts the blame game. "The woman whom you gave me to be with, she gave me of the tree, and I ate" (Genesis 3:12). Adam blamed God and the woman for his sin and Eve then blamed the serpent. From this time forward we find mankind rather than take responsibility for his choices tends to blame someone or something.

There are times when we sin we become fearful that God will not forgive us, which is a cruel deception for God declares that if we confess our sins He will forgive. Therefore the first step in getting things right with God when we sin is to admit the truth and take personal responsibility for our disobedience. Next is to confess what we have done and ask God to forgive us. Then remember1 John 1:9 assures us that God will forgive us and cleanse us from all unrighteousness.

The consequence of Adam and Eve sin was God expelling them from the Garden. However, if you end the story there you will fail to see the revelation of God's character and nature in handling their bad choices. In this account, you find God did not respond in anger or bitterness, nor did he retaliate by striking them with a bolt of lightning.

This is good news for someone who thinks of God being angry and carrying a big club to "whack" those who blow it. Instead of whacking Adam and Eve, God calls out to Adam to bring him out of his fearful hiding and confront his sin.

God's talking to Adam and Eve is like a loving parent dealing with a disobedient child who is trying to hide what he did. The parent knows what the child did, and because he loves his child, he will correct, instruct, and train him so that the child can become a successful adult.

In like manner, God knew what they had done, but he was willing to hear them out and then address their thinking and feelings. He wanted them to understand the consequence of their wrong choice. Furthermore, God desired to demonstrate He stilled loved them and understood their new shameful feelings.

God's love and compassion was further demonstrated when He made some designer clothes and clothed them so they would no longer be naked.

This revelation of God comforts me. It assures me that I don't have to be afraid and hide from God when I make wrong choices and blow it. I don't have to listen and believe the lies of the devil that God is going to get me or the accusations that I could not love God and be disobedient. The truth is that God understands our human nature because Jesus as a man had to deal with life just as we do.

When you consider how God handled Adam and Eve's sin it will also change your attitude towards mistakes of others. It is not Godly to let your disappointment in others wrong choices create emotions of anger, bitterness, harshness, and retaliation. Proverbs 10:12 states, "Hatred stirs up strife, but love covers all sins."

Thus, as you matured and understand more clearly the fears and feelings that lead one to make wrong choices, you will choose to help them and cover their nakedness rather than gossip about it. In showing them God's love you will experience the truth of James 5:20, "Let him know that he who turns a sinner from the error of his way will save a soul from death and cover a multitude of sins."

God's problem with mankind, from the time Adam and Eve sinned, has been the deception that the tree of knowledge of good and evil has answers about life rather than the tree of life.

The state of Adam's mind before he sinned reveals man's knowledge, although awesome in this day and time, is not even close to what it could be.

We read in Genesis 2:19-20, "Out of the ground the LORD God formed every beast of the field and every bird of the air, and brought *them* to Adam to see what he would call them. And whatever Adam called each living creature that *was* its name. So Adam gave names to all cattle, to the birds of the air, and to every beast of the field. But for Adam there was not found a helper comparable to him." In creating their names Adam is exercising the authority God had given him. Furthermore he must also remember their names so the animals would know whom Adam was calling. This is mind blowing. No Biology professor of today could come close to remembering the names for thousands of species.

It is man's ability to think and reason that sets him apart from all other creatures. Mathematics is an exact science, that makes so much possible and yet there is much that cannot be measured. An elephant does not know how long his trunk is in feet and inches. A monkey does not know how long his broad jump is. A squirrel does not know the circumference of a tree. Man, however, can measure speed and distance. He knows exactly how far it is to the moon and back. Man can also visualize a bridge over a river and then build it.

God created man with the ability to achieve and invent new things and we live in a wonderful age of knowledge and technology. For example, we can now do things with the aide of the computer that once was impossible. It is a sign of our greatness and superiority. But we are still not at the stage God intends to bring us.

Adam and Eve's sin demonstrates the truth you have freedom of choice but you do not have freedom of consequence. They thought knowledge would make them gods but it did not. Here are some of the consequences to their disobedience:

- Their eyes were opened and they lost their innocence.
- They were expelled from the Garden. Just as there was no place found in heaven for Satan due to his sin, there is likewise no place found in the Garden of Eden for Adam and Eve, due to their sin. And there will be no place in heaven for us if our sins are not forgiven through the blood of Jesus.
- They were limited to "natural" knowledge. By this I mean knowledge that only deals with the natural and physical realms, and not supernatural, and/or revelation knowledge.
- They released sin and death into the world.
- They transferred their authority and dominion over earth to Satan and God was no longer their God for Scripture declare that whomever you obey, that's who your God is (Romans 6:16).

Once their authority was given to Satan, he proceeded to establish his kingdom, called the "kingdom of darkness" and referred to as "the world". We will see the effects of this in our next chapter.

FIVE

The Evil Empire

Jesus made a statement in John 12:31 that has such profound meaning that I wonder why the subject is not taught more often: "Now is the judgment of this world, now shall the prince of this world be cast out. And I, if I be lifted up from this earth will draw all men unto me." Jesus said the time for the world to be judged and the prince of the world cast out had come.

You will find very little about the world in the Old Testament. But in the New Testament, an explosion occurs on the subject, especially in the writings of the Apostle John. For example, he states that if you love the world, the love of the Father is not in you (1 John 2:15-17). And again in James 4:4, we are told if you love the world, you are an enemy of God.

If you do not understand what Jesus is addressing, you can be confused about why God commands you to love not the world and in one of the most often quoted verses of the Bible states "For God so loved the world that He gave his only son, that whoever believes in Him should not perish but have everlasting life" (John 3:16).

The Greek word for world is *Kosmos*, which has three different dimensions. As we look at these three dimensions, you will begin to comprehend the idea of *loving* and *not loving* the world. In the classical Greek, *Kosmos* means two things: (1) primarily order or arrangement, and (2) an embellishment, or adornment. The New Testament writers reveal that *Kosmos* consists primarily of three entities—the material universe, the earth's occupants, and finally the affairs therein.

The material universe includes the physical, round world and according to Acts 17:24 God made the world and all things that are in it. This reference to "world" is the physical world as it relates to our universe.

The second meaning encapsulated in *Kosmos* is the people who inhabit the earth. For example, John 1:10 states, "Jesus came into the world, and the world knew him not." *World* in this sense is not referring to the material world, but to the inhabitants of the world. In John 3:16 *world* is speaking of all mankind, who are alienated from God and hostile to the cause of Jesus.

Examples of the *world* used as a collective "people" is also found in Hebrews 11:38, where it is stated that the world was not worthy of Jesus, John 14:17 references Jesus as someone "whom the world cannot receive," and in John 15:18, the world hates Jesus and the world will also hate you if you are a follower of Him.

The third category in which *Kosmos* falls into is worldly affairs. This includes the whole circle of worldly goods, endowments, riches, advantages, and leisure. Though hollow and fleeting, these things are designed to stir our desire and seduce us from God. Thus we are asked in Matthew 16:26 with regards to the tangible things of the world, "What would it prosper a man, if he should gain the whole world, and lose his soul?"

The material world can also refer to abstract things that have a spiritual value. For example, in 1 Corinthians 2:12 we learn, "God has not given us of the spirit of the world," and in 1 Corinthians 3:19, "The wisdom of the world is foolish to God." We are told in Titus 2:12 to say "no to ungodliness and worldly passions (lust)." In James 1:27 Christians are told to keep themselves unspotted from the *world.*

Let me remind you of a powerful truth, the devil is not God, he can not be in every place all the time as revealed in Job 1:7 when Satan comes into the presence of God and is asked where he has been he replies he has been walking to and fro across this earth. Therefore if Satan is going to rule the earth he must establish a system by which he can govern and control. The system he established is called the world.

The apostle John, in 1 John 5:19, reveals that behind the physical and natural dimensions of this world an invisible intangible element is present, "We know that we are of God, and the whole world lies under the sway of the wicked one." I call it "The Evil Empire."

This Evil Empire is anti-Christ and hostile to everything of God and of His kingdom. This is why Jesus said that He is not of the world, and commands us to overcome the world. There is an evil mind and personality called Satan behind this *Kosmos,* or organized system. John writes in 1 John 5:4-5 that, "you can overcome the world if your faith is in Jesus." And in 1 John 4:4 gives the reason; "because He who is in you is greater than he who is in the world."

In Genesis after the fall of Adam and Eve things really changed on earth as seen in the two sons of Adam and Eve, Cain and Abel. It is recorded that in due time they both brought an offering to the Lord. Cain brought an offering of fruit and Abel brought the firstborn of his flock. God accepted Abel's offering and rejected Cain's. Cain became so angry that he murdered Able. This began the shedding of innocent blood by Satan that has accelerated in these last days.

The Apostle John makes a startling statement about this event in 1 John 3:12, "not as Cain who was of the wicked one and murdered his brother. Why did he murder him? Because his works were evil and his brother's righteous." And Jesus declared in John 8:44, "You are of your father the devil, and the desires of your father you want to do. He was a murderer from the beginning, and does not stand in the truth, because there is no truth in him. When he speaks a lie, he speaks from his own resources, for he is a liar and the father of it."

There is an innocent sounding statement in Genesis 4:22 about a forger of cutting instruments of brass and iron. I dare say that a few centuries ago, if someone had said there's a spirit of Satan in those instruments, everyone would sarcastically ask "what's wrong with brass and iron?" Today we have the benefit of knowing what's wrong with brass and iron, when it's in the hand of an evil one they become weapons to kill and instruments of war.

We have come a long way since Cain murdered Able; in this present generation the world is filled with violence and bloodshed from the slaughter of babies still in the womb to parents murdering their children and children murdering their parents, gang killings, drive by shootings, road rage and home invasions, to mention a few.

Because Satan is in control everything that is called the world and its system is totally evil, thus it corrupts everything it touches and this is why God hates it. In fact if you take anything that's in the world—anything you want, you will find that even if it starts out with good intentions it eventually becomes corrupt and has an evil influence.

Television, for example, began as a naive benign means to strengthen the moral fiber of our nation with programs like, "The Brady Family", "Father Knows Best", and "Leave It To Beaver". Now we have "Desperate Housewives", "The Family Guy", and "Sex in The City".

The sad news is that television is now the number one babysitter and by the time a child reaches high school he witnessed 33,000 TV murders and 200,000 acts of violence according to Common Cause report in the 1995 May/Spring issue. In January 1998 an article in USA Today reported that in a single year in America the average sixteen year old will witness 16,000 sex acts reference on TV, and parents wonder why their children go astray.

The world will always produce depravity because by its nature it is an evil system it. Take worldly music as an example. MTV and VH1 started out as mild rock video and now almost everything they do involves sex, drugs, and rebellion.

Cartoons and children books are further examples. They use to be innocence nursery rhymes such as "little Red Riding Hood," but now they teach young children to rebel or that it is okay to have two mommies or two daddies.

The advent of video games has opened up a new wave of rebellion, sex, and violence as they program the mind to kill and destroy.

Consider the unprincipled methods used in our educational system. Did you know that all earlier state college institutions started out as Christian institutions whose presidents where usually Christian preachers. Their primary purpose was to train ministers to preach the gospel. If you visit one now, you'll find quite the opposite is true—they promote everything but Christianity.

In a US News and World Report of November 8, 1983 it was reported that 3 million crimes per year are committed in or near public schools. In March, 2001, Psychology In The Schools, reported 9% of eight graders carry a gun, knife or club to school at least once a month and estimated 275,000 guns go to school every day.

One major cause of our educational system becoming inept at teaching but experts in corrupting the morals of students began in 1963 when prayer in school was declared illegal. I Googled the subject of removing prayer from schools and found this article in All About History;

School prayer was the focus of Madalyn Murray O'Hair, a militant left wing atheist with close ties to the American Communist Party, when she filed a lawsuit against the school board of Baltimore. The local court judge, J. Gilbert Pendergast, dismissed the petition stating, "It is abundantly clear that petitioners' real objective is to drive every concept of religion out of the public school system." The case went to the Maryland Court of Appeals, and the court ruled, "Neither the First nor the Fourteenth Amendment was intended to stifle all rapport between religion and government."

The "School Prayer" case then made its way to the U.S. Supreme Court. Leonard Kerpelman addressed the court saying prayer in the public schools had been tolerated for so long that it had become traditional and that anything that is unconstitutional does not become constitutional through tradition. He went on to say the Constitution had erected a "wall of separation" between church and state, at which point Justice Potter Steward interrupted, asking where this wording appears. Kerpelman was stumped and an embarrassing silence followed. When he regained his composure, he stated that the text was not explicit on the point but that it had been interpreted to mean so.

Remarkably, the National Council of Churches and several Jewish organizations favored Madalyn O'Hair's case! Not a single Christian organization filed a brief in support of school prayer. The Supreme Court ruled 8 to 1 in favor of abolishing school prayer and Bible reading in the public schools. Justice Tom Clark wrote, "Religious freedom, it has long been recognized that government must be neutral and, while protecting all, must prefer none and disparage none." The federal government considers atheism to be a religion, and this Supreme Court ruling favored atheism, at the expense of the Christian majority.

It is now evident that anything that belongs to the world—Government, politics, and medicine—they all are under the control of Satan. Even with so much science and technology because of the corruption of his mind, man still is unable to draw the line where good stops and evil begins.

And that's why man's inventions eventually produce evil. Let's take commerce as another example. In Ezekiel 28, Satan is identified as being one who traffics in commerce. In Revelations 18, the center of commerce is shown to be the harlot's city of Babylon, and we are told it corrupts everything and will have a great fall. If you don't think commerce is corrupt go into different parts of the world and see all the evil and corruption it has produced through magazines, movies, videos, music, and the Internet. Pornographic material, for example, use to be restricted to magazines hidden behind the counter. Now you can watch it on TV and the Internet right in your living room. I have yet to figure out what a near nude woman has to do with advertising toothpaste other than lust is appealing.

We began this chapter with the good news of John 12:31 "Now is the judgment of this world, now shall the prince of this world be cast out. And I, if I be lifted up from this earth will draw all men unto me."

Now let me tell you why it is good for you to know Jesus has already judged this system and that it is bankrupt. A few years ago a large company named Enron dominated the news—it had gone *bankrupt* due to corrupt managers. Thousands of people and business lost millions of dollars. But I have some good news; a once in a lifetime opportunity for you! I bought some Enron stock for $120.00 a share and now I am willing to sell this stock for $50 a share. Think about it. You can buy stock I paid $120 for only $50.

How many would you buy? None!

Okay, just because I like you, I will come down to $25? Now how many would you buy? None!

Okay, I'll tell you what I'll do, I'll sell it to you for $5 a share, then you can sell it to someone and make a fortune since I paid $120 per share. Now how many would you like? None!

Do you understand what is happening here? You can buy stock that I bought for $120 for only $5! So why will you not buy the stock?

It's WHAT?! It's *worthless*?!

Likewise the world, just like Enron, is worthless. The Bible says very clearly the world is passing away and the only thing that will remain is he that does the will of God! So here is a litmus test for you. Have you been delivered from the world or are you still investing your life in things of the world rather than seeking first the kingdom of God and his righteousness?

Here is a truth worth remembering; "You will live longer after you die regardless of how long you live in this world." Therefore, "Do not lay up for yourselves treasures on earth, where moth and rust destroy and where thieves break in and steal; "but lay up for yourselves treasures in heaven, where neither moth nor rust destroys and where thieves do not break in and steal" (Matthew 6:19-20).

SECOND D

SIX

Jesus the Son of God

The Bible reveals Jesus was always upsetting someone and it is still true today. Jesus knew He was controversial and asked His disciples, "'Who do men say that I, the Son of Man, am?' So they said, 'Some *say* John the Baptist, some Elijah, and others Jeremiah or one of the prophets.' He said to them, 'But who do you say that I am?' Simon Peter answered and said, 'You are the Christ, the Son of the living God.' Jesus answered and said to him, "'Blessed are you, Simon Bar-Jonah, for flesh and blood has not revealed *this* to you, but My Father who is in heaven'"(Matthew 16:13-17).

Several years ago there was a TV show that consisted of three contestants. One person had an unusual hobby or work, and the other two people pretended to be this person. A panel of celebrities would ask questions of the three contestants with the goal of choosing the real person. They would then choose one of the contestants and give the reason for their choice. The host would then say, "Will the real Mr. (Smith) please stand up?" Sometimes the entire panel would get the right one. Sometimes there would be a mixture of choices and sometimes they would miss altogether.

This show reminds me of where the church is today with regard to the real Jesus. There is a Protestant Jesus, a Catholic Jesus, A Mormon Jesus, A Jehovah Witness Jesus, a Charismatic Jesus, and a Pentecostal Jesus. Then there is *your* Jesus. So will the real Jesus please stand up?

This is very important issue because Christianity is based on the life, character, and identity of Jesus, who did not come to teach Christianity he is Christianity. Thus Christianity is not a religion but a personal relationship through Jesus, with the God who created us to be his family.

Religions, on the other hand are based on philosophy or theological ideologies. If you remove the founder or guru from these religions they will essentially remain intact, because they are based on the teachings of and not upon the founder himself. But if you remove Jesus from Christianity you no longer have Christianity. Otherwise you could rightly consider other beliefs and teachings might be just as valid as Christianity.

Here is how the Apostle Paul addressed this issue many years ago for people who were not sure about Jesus in 1 Corinthians 15: 12-22, "Now if it be preached that Christ has been raised from the dead, how can some among you say that there is no resurrection of the dead? If there be no resurrection of the dead, then not even Christ has been raised. And if Christ were not raised, our preaching is useless and so is your faith. More than that we are found to be false witnesses about God, for we have testified about God that he raised Christ from the dead. But he did not raise him if in fact the dead are not raised. For if the dead are not raised, then Christ has not been raised either. And if Christ has not been raised, your faith is vain; you are still in your sins. Then those also who have fallen asleep in Christ are lost. If only for this life we have hope in Christ, we are to be pitted more than all men. But Christ has been raised from the dead; the first fruits of those who have fallen asleep. For since death came through a man, the resurrection of the dead also comes through a man. For as in Adam all die, so in Christ all will be made alive."

In this passage, the Apostle Paul states that Christianity is based upon the resurrection of Jesus. If, therefore, Jesus did not rise from the grave Christianity is just another hopeless religion. No other religion, however, claims the leader they worship and follow is alive today because those founders all died and are still dead. It is, therefore, the resurrection of Jesus that is the ultimate proof that Jesus was God in the flesh.

But what is the evidence that it really happened? I want to summarize the evidence under four main headings:

1. **His absence from the tomb**. Many theories have been put forward to explain the fact that Jesus' body was absent from the tomb on the first Easter Day, but none of them is very convincing. First, it has been suggested that Jesus did not die on the cross. Jesus had undergone Roman flogging under which many had died, and then was nailed to a cross for six hours. Could man in this condition push away a stone weighing probably a ton and a half?

    Furthermore, when the soldiers discovered that Jesus was already dead, "one of the soldiers pierced Jesus' side with a spear, bringing a sudden flow of blood and water" (John 19:34). This appears to be the separation of clot and serum, which we know today, is strong medical evidence that Jesus was dead. John would not have possessed that knowledge, which makes it even more powerful evidence that Jesus was indeed dead.

    Secondly, it has been argued that the disciples stole the body. Some have suggested that the disciples stole the body and began a rumor that Jesus had raised from the dead. Leaving aside the fact that the tomb was guarded, this theory is psychologically improbable. The disciples were depressed and disillusioned at the time of Jesus death. There would have to have been something extraordinary to transform the apostle Peter into the man who preached at Pentecost where three thousand people were converted.

    In addition, when one considered how much they had to suffer for what they believed (floggings, torture, and for some even death), it seems inconceivable that they would be prepared to endure that for something they knew to be untrue.

Thirdly, some have said that the authorities stole the body. This seems the least probable theory of all. If the authorities had stolen the body, why did they not produce it when they were trying to quash the rumor that Jesus had raised from the dead?

2. **His appearances to the disciples**. Were these hallucinations? The Concise Oxford Dictionary describes a hallucination as an "apparent perception of external object not actually present." Hallucinations normally occur in highly-strung, highly imaginative, and very nervous people, or in people who are sick or on drugs. The disciples do not fit into any of these categories. Burly fishermen, tax collector, and skeptics like Thomas are unlikely to hallucinate. People who hallucinate would be unlikely to suddenly stop doing so. Jesus appeared to His disciples on eleven different occasions over a period of six weeks. The number of occasions and the sudden cessation make the hallucination theory highly improbable.

    Furthermore over 500 people saw the risen Jesus. It is possible for one person to hallucinate. Maybe it is possible for two or three people to share the same hallucination. But is it likely that 500 people would all share the same hallucination? And finally, hallucinations are subjective; like seeing a ghost.

    Jesus could be and was touched physically. He ate a piece of broiled fish (Luke 24:42-43) and on one occasion He cooked breakfast for the disciples (John 21:1-14). Peter says, "(They) ate and drank with him after he rose from the dead" (Acts 10:41). He held long conversations with them, teaching them many things about the kingdom of God (Acts 1:3).

    The Bible records these appearances of Jesus after he had risen from the dead:

    •   In Mark 16:9-14 Jesus appeared to Mary Magdalene early the first morning. Then he appeared to two disciples walking in the country and later to his eleven apostles.

- In Matt. 28: 9-10 he appeared to other women on the first morning
- In Luke 24: 13-34 he appeared to two men on their way to Emmaus and also to Peter.
- In John 20:19 he appeared to ten apostles with Thomas being absent.
- Eight days later in John 20: 26-31 with Thomas present he again appeared to the apostles.
- In John 21:1-14 he appeared to seven apostles by the Sea of Galilee.
- In Matthew 28: 16-20 he appeared to the eleven apostles in Galilee.
- In 1 Corinthians 15:5-8 he appeared to Cephas, to the twelve, to Peter, to more than 500, to James, and also to Paul.

These may not be the only appearances as Luke wrote in Acts that Jesus presented himself as being alive with many infallible proofs.

3. **The refusal of the Christians to renounce His resurrection.** It is known from historical records outside of Scripture that the sect named Christians came into existence in the reign of Tiberius, and the thing that brought them into existence was their belief that Jesus had risen from the dead.

Traditional history also records how various ones suffered cruel deaths because they preached Jesus was alive and the only Lord and Savior, and refused to change their confession in the face of certain death.

- Philip was scourged and crucified
- Matthew was nailed to the ground with spikes and beheaded.
- Simon was tortured and crucified.
- John the son of Zebedee was tortured and exiled.

- James the brother of John was beheaded.
- James, the brother of Jesus, was pushed from the top of a building and then his broken body was beaten to death.
- Peter's brother Andrew, hung on a cross three days before dying.
- Bartholomew was beaten and skinned alive before being beheaded.
- Thomas was speared with a javelin.
- Peter was crucified upside down.

It seems to me that if all these people claiming they had seen Jesus were lying; or if the body had been stolen, sooner or latter the truth would have come out. Especially when you consider none really expected Jesus to rise from the grave and they all were willing to die without ever admitting the whole thing was a hoax. I think at least one would not be willing to die for something he knew was a hoax.

4. **Historical writings.** That Jesus was a person who lived and died is supported by a great deal of evidence from the gospels and other Christian writings, and also from non-Christian sources. For example, the Roman historians Tacitus (directly) and Suetonius (indirectly) both wrote about him.

Here is how the Jewish historian Josephus, born in 37 AD describes Jesus and his followers thus; "Now there was about this time, Jesus, a wise man, if it be lawful to call him a man, for he was a doer of wonderful works, a teacher of such men as receive the truth with pleasure. He drew over to him both many of the Jews, and many of the Gentiles. He was (the) Christ; and when Pilate, at the suggestion of the principal men amongst us, had condemned him to the cross, those that loved him at first did not forsake him, for he appeared to them alive again the third day, as the divine prophets had foretold these and ten thousand other wonderful things concerning him; and the tribe of Christians so named after him, are not extinct at this day." (Books 18 and 20).

So there is evidence outside the Bible for the existence of Jesus. And the evidence in the New Testament is very strong. But some may say, 'The New Testament was written a long time ago. How do we know that what they wrote down is true or has not been changed over the years?" The answer is that we do know, very accurately through the science of textual criticism, what the New Testament writers wrote. F.F. Bruce (The New Testament Documents: Are they Reliable? By F. F. Bruce, 1943) points out that for Caesar's Gallic War we have nine or ten copies and the oldest was written some nine hundred years later in Caesar's day. For Livy's Roman *History* we have not more than twenty copies, the earliest of which comes from around 900 A.D. Of the fourteen books of the histories of Tacitus, only twenty copies survive. Of the sixteen books of his Annals, ten portions of his two great historical works depend entirely on two manuscripts, one from the ninth century, and one from the eleventh century. The history of Thucydides is known almost entirely from eight manuscripts from about 900 A.D. The same is true of the history of Herodotus. Yet no classical scholar doubts the authenticity of these works, in spite of the large time gap and the relatively few manuscripts.

As regards the New Testament we have a great wealth of material. The New Testament was probably written between 40 and 100 A. D. We have excellent full manuscripts of the whole New Testament dating from as early as 350 A.D. (a time span of only three hundred years), papyri containing most of the New Testament writings dating from the third century and even a fragment of John's Gospel dating from about 130 A.D. If you visit the Holy Land Experience in Orlando you can see some of the clay and papyri writings from this time era. There are over five thousand Greek manuscripts, over ten thousand Latin manuscripts,

9,300 other manuscripts, as well as over thirty-six thousand citing in the writings of the early church fathers.

Essentially, the more texts we have discovered the less doubt there is about the accuracy of the Scripture. F. F. Bruce summarizes the evidence by quoting Sir Fredric Kenyon, a leading scholar in this area: the interval then between the dates of original composition and the earliest extant evidence becomes so small as to be in fact negligible, and the last foundation for any doubt that the Scriptures have come down to us substantially as they were written has now been removed. Both the authenticity and the general integrity of the books of the New Testament may be regarded as finally established.

Some people say, "Jesus never claimed to be God." Indeed, it is true that Jesus did not go around saying the words, "I am God." Yet when one looks at all He taught and claimed, there is little doubt that He was conscious of being a man whose identity was God.

Jesus said a number of things, which, although not direct claims to be God, show that He regarded Himself as being in the same position as God, as seen in the following examples:

His Authority to forgive sins. Jesus' claim to be able to forgive sins is well known. For example, on one occasion He said to a man who was paralyzed, "Son, your sins are forgiven" (Mark 2:5). The reaction of religious leaders was, "Why does this fellow talk like that? He's blaspheming! Who can forgive sins but God alone?" Jesus went on to prove that He did have the authority to forgive sins by healing a paralyzed man. His claim to be able to forgive sins is indeed an astonishing claim.

C. S. Lewis puts it well when he says in his book *Mere Christianity:* "One part of the claim tends to slip past us unnoticed because we have heard it so often that we no longer see what it amounts to. I mean the claim to forgive sins: any sins. Now unless the speaker is God, this is really so preposterous as to be comic. We can all understand how a man forgives offenses against himself. You tread on my toe and I forgive you, you steal my money and I forgive you. But what should we make of a man, himself unrobed and untrodden on, who announced that he forgave you for treading on other men's toes and stealing other men's money? Asinine fatuity is the kindest description we should give of his conduct. Yet this is what Jesus did. He told people that their sins were forgiven, and never waited to consult all the other people whom their sins had undoubtedly injured. He unhesitatingly behaved as if He was the party chiefly concerned, the person chiefly offended in all offenses."

This makes sense only if He really was the God whose laws are broken and whose love is wounded in every sin. In the mouth of any speaker who is not God, these words would imply what I can only regard as a silliness and conceit unrivaled by any other character in history.

He would Judge the world. Another extraordinary claim that Jesus made was that one day He would return and "sit on his throne in heavenly glory." All the nations would be gathered before Him and He would pass judgment on them. Some would receive an inheritance prepared for them since the creation of the world and eternal life, while others would suffer the punishment of being separated from Him forever. Jesus also said He be would the judge, and the criterion of judgment. Thus what happens to us on the Day of Judgment depends on how we respond to Jesus in this life (Matthew 25:31-45).

The Apostle Paul confirmed this truth to the Athenians in Acts 17:31, "because He has appointed a day on which He will judge the world in righteousness by the Man whom He has ordained. He has given assurance of this to all by raising Him from the dead."

He allowed people to worship Him. One time Jesus accepted the invitation of a Pharisee to visit. While he was there a woman came in and in an act of humility and worship washed his feet with her tears and anointed them with oil. Jesus did not rebuke her and say you are only to worship God as seen in

Luke 7:37-38, "And behold, a woman in the city who was a sinner, when she knew that Jesus sat at the table in the Pharisee's house, brought an alabaster flask of fragrant oil, and stood at His feet behind Him weeping; and she began to wash His feet with her tears, and wiped *them* with the hair of her head; and she kissed His feet and anointed them with the fragrant oil."

His direct claims. In the gospel of Mark's record of Jesus trial when the question was put to him, "Are you the Christ, the Son of the Blessed One?" Jesus said, "'I am . . . and you will see the Son of Man sitting at the right hand of the Mighty One and coming on the clouds of heaven.' The high priest tore his clothes. 'Why do we need any more witnesses?' he asked. 'You have heard the blasphemy. What do you think'" (Mark 14:61-64)? In this account, it appears Jesus was condemned to death for the assertion He made about Himself. A claim tantamount to a claim to be God was blasphemy in Jewish eyes, worthy of death.

On one occasion, when the Jews started to stone Jesus, He asked, "Why are you stoning me?" They replied they were stoning Him for blasphemy "'because you, a mere man, claim to *be God*'"(John 10:33, italics added). His enemies clearly thought that He was declaring to be God.

When Thomas, one of His disciples, knelt down before Jesus and said, "My Lord and my God" (John 20:28), Jesus didn't turn to him and say, "No, no, don't say that; I am not God." He said, "Because you have seen me, you have believed; blessed are those who have not seen and yet have believed" (John 20:29).

The demons recognized who he was as seen by this authority over them and how they spoke to him a seen in Matthew 8:28-29, "When He had come to the other side, to the country of the Gergesenes, there met Him two demon-possessed *men*, coming out of the tombs, exceedingly fierce, so that no one could pass that way. And suddenly they cried out, saying, "What have we to do with You, Jesus, You Son of God? Have You come here to torment us before the time?"

Jesus claim to be the unique Son of God and God made flesh needs to be tested. People make all kinds of claims and the mere fact that somebody claims to be someone does not mean the claim is right. Many people, some in psychiatric hospitals, are deluded. They think they are Napoleon or the Pope, but they are not. So how can we test his claims?

There are three logical possibilities. The first would be the claim is either true or untrue. If the claims were untrue, either He knew they were untrue, in which case He was an imposter, and an evil one at that. Or, secondly, He did not know, in which case He was deluded; indeed, He was mad. The third possibility is that the claims were true.

In order to assess which of these three possibilities is right let's examine some evidence that we have about His life.

His teachings. Jesus' teachings are the foundation of our entire civilization in the West and are considered to be the greatest teaching that has ever fallen from anyone's lips. Many of the laws in England and North America were originally based on the teachings of Jesus.

One of the fascinating things about Jesus is that so much of His teaching was centered on Himself. He said to people, in effect, "If you want to have a relationship with God, you need to come to me" (see John 14:6). It's through a relationship with Him that we encounter God.

We are making progress in virtually every field of science and technology, and yet in nearly two thousand years no one has improved on the moral teaching of Jesus Christ.

The human heart has a deep hunger to be loved, to be accepted, and to be secure. The leading psychologists of the twentieth century have all recognized this. Freud said, "People are hungry for love." Jung said, "People are hungry for security." Adler said, "People are hungry for significance." Jesus said, "I am the bread of life" (John 6:35). In other words, "If you want your hunger satisfied, come to me."

Many people in our society are walking in darkness, depression, disillusionment, and despair. They are looking for direction. Jesus said, "I am the light of the world. Whoever follows me will never walk in darkness, but will have the light of life" (John 8:12).

Many are fearful of death. Jesus said, "I am the resurrection and the life. He who believes in me will live, even though he dies; and whoever lives and believes in me will never die" (John 11:25-26)

Many are burdened by worries, anxieties, fears, and guilt. Jesus said, "Come to me, all you who are weary and burdened, and I will give you rest" (Matt 11:28).

Many are not sure how to run their lives or whom they should follow. Jesus said, "Follow me (Mark 1:17).

Philip, one of His disciples, wanted to see the Father and Jesus asked him, "Have I been with you so long, and yet you have not known Me, Philip? He who has seen Me has seen the Father; so how can you say, 'Show us the Father?" Jesus said in effect; if you want to know what God looks like, look at me (John 14:9).

His works. In answering the charge of blasphemy Jesus said, "Do you say of Him whom the Father sanctified and sent into the world, 'You are blaspheming,' because I said, 'I am the Son of God'? If I do not do the works of My Father, do not believe Me; but if I do, though you do not believe Me, believe the works, that you may know and believe that the Father is in Me, and I in Him" (John 10:36-38).

There are many works that demonstrate Jesus was who he claimed to be. For instance, He received one person's picnic and multiplied it so that he could feed thousands (Mark 6:30-44). He had control over the elements and could speak to the wind and the waves and thereby stop a storm (Mark 4:35-41). He carried out the most remarkable healings: opening blind eyes, causing the deaf and dumb to hear and speak, and enabling the paralyzed to walk again. A man who had been an invalid for thirty-eight years was able to pick up his bed and walk (John 5:1-9). He set people free from evil forces that had dominated their lives. On occasion, He even brought those who had died back to life (John 11:38-44).

Yet it was not just His miracles that made His work so impressive. It was His love, especially for the loveless (for instance, the lepers and the prostitutes), that seemed to motivate all that He did.

If you have seen the Passion of Christ movie you saw and experienced his supreme work of love was shown on the cross. When they tortured Him and nailed Him to the cross, He said, "Father, forgive them, for they do not know what they are doing" (Luke 23:34). Surely these are not the activities of an evil or deluded man?

His character. Jesus was a man who exemplified supreme unselfishness but never self-pity; humility but not weakness; joy but never at another's expense; kindness but not indulgence. He was a man in whom even His enemies could find no fault and where friends who knew him well said He was without sin. Surely no one could suggest that a man with a character like that was evil or unbalanced?

His fulfillment of Old Testament prophesies. Wilbur Smith, the American writer on theological topics, said: "The ancient world had many different devices for determining the future, known as divination, but not in the entire gamut of Greek and Latin literature, even though they used the words prophet and prophecy, can we find any real specific prophecy of a great historic event to come in the distant future, nor any prophecy of a Savior to arrive in the human race ... Mohammedanism cannot point to any prophecies of the coming of Mohammed uttered hundreds of years before his birth. Neither can the founders of any cult in this country rightly identify any ancient text specifically foretelling their appearance."

Yet in the case of Jesus, He fulfilled over three hundred prophecies (spoken by different voices over five hundred years), including twenty-nine major prophecies fulfilled in a single day—the day He died. Although some of these prophecies may have found fulfillment at one level in the prophet's own day, they found their ultimate fulfillment in Jesus Christ.

I suppose it could be suggested that Jesus was a clever con man who deliberately set out to fulfill these prophecies in order to show that He was the Messiah foretold in the Old Testament. The problem with this suggestion is, first, the sheer number of them would have made it extremely difficult. Secondly, humanly speaking He had no control over many of the events.

For example, the exact manner of His death was foretold in the Old Testament (Isaiah 53), and also the place of His burial and even the place of His birth (Micah 5:2). Suppose Jesus had been a con man wanting to fulfill all these prophecies. It would have been a bit late by the time He discovered the place in which He was supposed to have been born!

It only took about three hundred years for the witness of uneducated fishermen and tax gatherers, to sweep across the whole known world, proclaiming Jesus was the resurrected Messiah.

The books of the New Testament are a perfectly amazing story of a peaceful revolution that has no parallel in the history of the world. It came about because Christians were able to say to inquirers: "Jesus not only died for you. He is alive! You can meet him and discover for yourself the reality we are talking about!" Many did, and joined the church and the church, born from that Easter grave, spread everywhere.

Countless millions of people down through the ages have experienced the risen Christ. They consist of people of every color, race, tribe, nationality, social, economic, and intellectual backgrounds. Yet they all unite in a common experience of the risen Christ.

There are some who do not realize there have only been two men on earth as revealed in 1 Corinthians 15:45-50, "and so it is written, "The first man Adam became a living being." The last Adam became a life-giving spirit. However, the spiritual is not first, but the natural, and afterward the spiritual. The first man was of the earth, made of dust; the second Man is the Lord from heaven. As was the man of dust, so also are those who are made of dust; and as is the heavenly Man, so also are those who are heavenly. And as we have borne the image of the man of dust, we shall also bear the image of the heavenly Man. Now this I say, brethren, that flesh and blood cannot inherit the kingdom of God; nor does corruption inherit incorruption."

Here we are told that we have borne the image of Adam, referring to Genesis 5:1-3, "This is the book of the genealogy of Adam. In the day that God created man, He made him in the likeness of God. He created them male and female, and blessed them and called them Mankind in the day they were created. And Adam lived one hundred and thirty years, and *begot a son in his own likeness*, after his image, and named him Seth" (Emphasis added). Note that after Adam sinned he was no longer in the image of God; therefore his children bore his image and not the image of God.

This helps explain why Jesus had to be born of woman and could not be born of man. If Jesus had been born of man he would have been in the image of Adam not God. But being born by the Spirit of God we are told in Colossians 1:15-17, "*He is the image of the invisible God,* the firstborn over all creation. For by Him all things were created that are in heaven and that are on earth, visible and invisible, whether thrones or dominions or principalities or powers. All things were created through Him and for Him. And He is before all things, and in Him all things consist" (emphasis added).

Another spiritual truth revealed here is that flesh and blood cannot inherit the spiritual kingdom. Therefore if you remain a child of Adam, you cannot enter into heaven because you are of the flesh and not of the spirit. But if you are born again through Jesus, God is your Father and you are spiritually qualified to be in God's kingdom.

Let's examine how you can be born spiritually through Jesus and no longer be of the Adam family but be children of God. We read in Romans 10:8-10, "But what does it say? "The word is near you, in your mouth and in your heart" (that is, the word of faith which we preach): that if you confess with your mouth the Lord Jesus and believe in your heart that God has raised Him from the dead, you will be saved. For with the heart one believes unto righteousness, and with the mouth confession is made unto salvation."

We are told that we must first believe with our heart. Isn't it interesting the Holy Spirit emphasizes our heart, not our mind? This has to do with the reality that our mind only thinks and reasons naturally, and considers spiritual things to be foolish. Our heart represents the essence of our spirit being and is where we first receive spiritual truths. If we dare to acknowledge what the Holy Spirit has revealed to our heart, God will then give our mind revelation and understanding.

Once you believe with your heart and mind that Jesus is your Lord, you must do the next step and confess with your mouth unto salvation what you now believe.

The word "confess" means to acknowledge or avow; to publicly declare a belief in and adherence to; to declare to be true; to admit; to show by the effect; to prove; to agree with; assent; to concede; not to refuse; to promise; declare; speak out freely; to declare openly; to profess one's self the worshipper of one; to praise, celebrate, to admit or declare one's self guilty of what one is accused of.

Matthew 10:32-33, tells as another reason why our confession is required; "Whosoever therefore shall confess me before men, him will I confess also before my Father which is in heaven. But whosoever shall deny me before men, him will I also deny before my Father which is in heaven." Notice that Jesus declares our confession must be public. A public confession is a statement of our position, and a separation with the world.

After making this true confession, you may begin to have doubts if you really did get saved, especially when you do, say, or think anything ungodly. Remember therefore I John 1:9 "If we confess our sins, he is faithful and just to forgive us our sins, and to cleanse us from all unrighteousness." It is not enough to just believe God forgives you; you must confess (name) the wrong (sin) and ask God to forgive you.

You will know the instant you sin because the Holy Spirit and your conscience will tell you. It is also important to not debate or wait about confessing the wrong, as sin hardens the heart and separates you from God.

So immediately acknowledge the sin and ask forgiveness. In so doing, your fellowship with God is not broken.

As you obey this command, the mind will become a battlefield. You may think God would not forgive you for doing such a horrible thing. Or, you've done it one too many times and you think God is through with you. You may be enticed not to confess because God will really get you if you do (as if He doesn't already know what you did). If you confess and accept God's forgiveness you will discover there is no condemnation in Jesus and that you are forgiven.

Almost everyone has read or heard about John 3:16, "For God so loved the world that He gave His only begotten Son, that whoever believes in Him should not perish but have everlasting life." The death and resurrection of Jesus is God's supreme act of love to make it possible for you and me to experience all that God desired us to be and do when he created us.

Here is an interesting truth; because Jesus was sinless he could not die, as death is a result of sin. Thus he had to become sin in order to enter into death as seen in 2 Corinthians 5:21, "For He made Him who knew no sin to be sin for us, that we might become the righteousness of God in Him." In the moment Jesus became sin on the cross, he suffered all the consequences of sin—sickness, disease, pain, suffering, and poverty. We are told God did this that we might become the righteousness of God in Him.

Sin is also an entrance into the domain of Satan and demons. Thus when Jesus became sin he enters into the kingdom of Satan. We are told in 1 Corinthians 2:7-8, "But we speak the wisdom of God in a mystery, the hidden wisdom which God ordained before the ages for our glory, which none of the rulers of this age knew; for had they known, they would not have crucified the Lord of glory." This reveals the devil did not know the consequences of crucifying Jesus or he would never have done it. Satan, however, had used death to stop the prophets of God, so the devil and his followers believed Jesus could also be stopped through death.

Thus, they were very happy when they finally put Jesus to death because he had caused them more grief than any of the prophets. He preached the kingdom of God had come, he fed the hungry, he healed the sick, he raised the dead, and he cast out demons. In other words, Jesus was bad news, and the worse nightmare, for Satan and his demons.

What an indescribable moment Jesus' death must have been for them? After all, they were able to witness the One they despised over any other man bear all the sins of mankind when He became sin. They could see all the evil they had wrought upon the earth and mankind and now Jesus was being delivered into their hands. This is why we read the earth became dark during the last hours Jesus was on the cross (Luke 23:44-45).

The Apostle Peter in Acts 2:22-36 preached a powerful sermon to explain what the death and resurrection of Jesus had accomplished; "Men of Israel, hear these words: Jesus of Nazareth, a Man attested by God to you by miracles, wonders, and signs which God did through Him in your midst, as you yourselves also know—" Him, being delivered by the determined purpose and foreknowledge of God, you have taken by lawless hands, have crucified, and put to death; "whom God raised up, having loosed the pains of death, because it was not possible that He should be held by it. "For David says concerning Him: 'I foresaw the LORD always before my face, For He is at my right hand, that I may not be shaken. Therefore my heart rejoiced, and my tongue was glad; moreover my flesh also will rest in hope. For You will not leave my soul in Hades, nor will You allow Your Holy One to see corruption. You have made known to me the ways of life; You will make me full of joy in Your presence.' "Men and brethren, let me speak freely to you of the patriarch David, that he is both dead and buried, and his tomb is with us to this day. "Therefore, being a prophet, and knowing that God had sworn with an oath to him that of the fruit of his body, according to the flesh, He would raise up the Christ to sit on his throne, "he, foreseeing this, spoke concerning the resurrection of the Christ, that His soul was not left in Hades, nor did His flesh see corruption. "This Jesus God has raised up, of which we are all witnesses. 33 "Therefore being exalted to the right hand of God, and having received from the Father the promise of the Holy Spirit, He poured out this which you now see and hear. "For David did not ascend into the heavens, but he says himself: 'The LORD said to my Lord, "Sit at My right hand, Till I make Your enemies Your footstool."' "Therefore let all the house of Israel know assuredly that God has made this Jesus, whom you crucified, both Lord and Christ."

From this sermon we learn the death and resurrection of Jesus was a predetermined plan of God in order for Jesus to become Lord and Christ, i.e. the Messiah or anointed one. Death could not hold him and his body experienced no corruption but he did enter into the realm of hell.

Jesus was in Hell because He became sin for our sin. He stayed there until God, the supreme judge of the universe, declared our penalty had been paid and that we were justified. The word *Justifies* means, "to pardon and clear from all guilt and to accept as righteous."

Romans 4:25 reveals this truth about Jesus in hell, "who was delivered up because of our offenses, and was raised because of our justification."

Picture this: in the midst of Satan and demons triumphantly celebrating the horrible death of Jesus, God proclaims Jesus' justification for us was complete, then they hear a booming command that causes them to freeze in terror: "*TURN HIM LOOSE.*" Their cheering abruptly stops as they gape in disbelief as Jesus walks up to Satan and says, "I'll take those keys to death and hell." Revelation 1:17-18 records that Jesus still has those keys, "and when I saw Him, I fell at His feet as dead. But He laid His right hand on me, saying to me, "Do not be afraid; I am the First and the Last. "I am He who lives, and was dead, and behold, I am alive forevermore. Amen. And I have the keys of hell and of death."

Here is how it is recorded in Colossians 2: 13-15, "And you, being dead in your sins and the uncircumcision of your flesh, He has made alive together with Him, having forgiven you all trespasses, blotting out the handwriting of ordinances that was against us, which was contrary to us, and has taken it out of the way, nailing it to the cross. Having stripped rulers and authorities, He made a show of them publicly, triumphing over them in it." When Jesus rose up from the grave he became victorious over sin, death, and Satan.

Then he entered into the true heavenly Holy of Holies with his own blood; Hebrews 9: 24-26, "For Christ has not entered the holy places made with hands, which are copies of the true, but into heaven itself, now to appear in the presence of God for us; not that He should offer Himself often, as the high priest enters the Most Holy Place every year with blood of another— He then would have had to suffer often since the foundation of the world; but now, once at the end of the ages, He has appeared to put away sin by the sacrifice of Himself."

Under the first covenant only the High Priest could enter into the Holy of Holies with the blood of animals to meet with God and sprinkle it on the mercy seat for forgiveness for himself and the people.

Jesus, however, entered the real Holy of Holies with his own blood, and there at the true mercy seat he sprinkled his blood for the forgiveness of our sins. Therefore, it is only Christians who can make the claim that our sins have been forgiven.

Let's read the truth about what Jesus did for us in Romans 5:1-11; 17-21, "Therefore being justified by faith, we have peace with God through our Lord Jesus Christ: By whom also we have access by faith into this grace wherein we stand, and rejoice in hope of the glory of God. And not only (so), but we glory in tribulations also: knowing that tribulation works patience; And patience, experience; and experience, hope: And hope makes not ashamed; because the love of God is shed abroad in our hearts by the Holy Ghost which is given unto us. For when we were yet without strength, in due time Christ died for the ungodly. For scarcely for a righteous man will one die: yet per adventure for a good man some would even dare to die. But God commends his love toward us, in that, while we were yet sinners, Christ died for us. Much more then, being now justified by his blood, we shall be saved from wrath through him. For if, when we were enemies, we were reconciled to God by the death of his Son, much more, being reconciled, we shall be saved by his life. And not only (so), but we also joy in God through *our* Lord Jesus Christ, by whom we have now received the atonement. (. . . . For if by one man's offence death reigned by one; much more they which receive abundance of grace and of the gift of righteousness shall reign in Life by one, Jesus."

These Scriptures are very important because God has placed in everyone a drive that urges us to seek eternal life and freedom from the curse of sin. Adults seek for happiness; the young seek to be cool.

I was reminded of this one night when I watched part of *Night Line* on ABC. A young and older woman was in a rehab program seeking a way to be set free from the consequences of abuse and addiction. My heart broke over the reality they were deceived into thinking they could be helped by changing their environment and circumstances.

The drive to be free can cause one to use alcohol as a means to numb the pain and become a drunkard, another may attempt to escape through drugs and become a drug addict, another through pornography and sex, and another through money and power.

A French philosopher made a profound statement when he said, "Before we first set our hearts on any one thing, let us first examine how happy are those who already possess it." What man has failed to understand is that man is a spirit being. He has a soul and lives in a physical body. This lack of knowledge keeps one from realizing his dissatisfaction is a spiritual hunger and thirst, which cannot be satisfied by the natural things of life. The hunger pains cease only when contact is made with Jesus Christ and the acknowledgement of Him as Lord. When this happens, the taste and attractions of the world they once sought suddenly become undesirable.

It seems to me there is a major problem within the church that confuses those who are seeking reality. They hear a lot of preaching about the need for sins being forgiven, but see very little change in the lives of those who professes to be a Christian, other than becoming religious, self-righteous, and attending church more than them.

Let me demonstrate the truth in what I am saying by asking you a few questions. Answer each question as now or when you get to heaven.

1. When is there rest and peace with God?
2. When are we cleansed and our sins forgiven?
3. When do we become whole, complete, and blameless?
4. When do we enter into the presence of the Lord?
5. When do old things pass away?
6. When do we have dominion over sin?
7. Does the blood of Jesus only forgive some sins?
8. Is redemption metaphysical or is it a reality?

In thinking about these questions, I was reminded of an incident from my college days. I was given a liquid to analyze and record what elements were present. I very carefully tested the liquid and reported my results to my professor. He looked at my report and said, "You missed one. There was lead in the sample and you do not have it listed."

I protested there was not lead in the sample because I tested for lead, and it was negative. This did not deter him from marking my answer wrong. When I asked him why the lead did not show up in the test, he stated that he didn't know what I had done wrong, but he knew there was lead in the sample because he was the one who added it to the solution.

This really upset me and because I still had some of the sample I repeated the test. To my astonishment it tested positive for lead. I still don't know how I missed it the first time, but he was right—I did something wrong.

In like manner, if you are thinking you must wait until you get to heaven to have what the Bible promises you are being defeated through wrong thinking and wrong choosing. Thinking that you must wait denies what we have seen God accomplished through Jesus.

Let's examine this from Jude 24, "Now unto him that is able to keep you from falling, and to present (you) faultless before the presence of his glory with exceeding joy." We live in His presence now; we walk in his presence now. If Jesus cannot present us "now" with exceeding joy, He certainly cannot present us to God after death; He said on the cross it is finished. Nothing is left undone.

If death is required to cleanse us from sin and make us righteous, we are in a dilemma. The wages of sin is death, not righteousness. And the author of death is the devil (Hebrews 2:14). Therefore to believe we must wait until heaven to receive righteousness is declaring that God needs the devil to complete His redemptive work. This is why the teaching on purgatory and similar doctrines that deny all our sins are forgiven and reject that we are righteous with God keep people in bondage to the works of the flesh, the world, and the devil.

This belief is also in opposition to 2 Corinthians 5:17-19, "Therefore if any man (be) in Christ, (he is) a new creature: old things are passed away; behold, all things are become new. And all things (are) of God, who has reconciled us to himself by Jesus Christ, and has given to us the ministry of reconciliation; To wit, that God was in Christ, reconciling the world unto himself, not imputing their trespasses unto them; and has committed unto us the word of reconciliation." Here we learn that we are not a person who is a composition of past failures, hurts, and sins doomed to live out your days in misery trying to be a Christian. We are new creation folks. If you do not believe your sins are forgiven and done away with, and that you are a new creation it will keep you from obtaining lasting victory in your life, and stunt your faith. We are either a new creation or not.

We have either passed from death into life, or we deny the promise in John 5:24, "Most assuredly, I say to you, he who hears My word and believes in Him who sent Me has everlasting life, and shall not come into judgment, but has passed from death into life."

We have either been made righteous, or we deny the statement of transformation in 2 Corinthians 5:21, "For he has made him (to be) sin for us, who knew no sin; that we might be made the righteousness of God in him."

We are either holy or we deny His change in us described in Colossians 1:21, "And you, that were sometime alienated and enemies in (your) mind by wicked works, yet now has he reconciled in the body of his flesh through death, to present you holy and unblamable and unreproveable in his sight."

We are either free from sin or we are servants of it, as stated in Romans 6:14, 17-18, "For sin shall not have dominion over you: for ye are not under the law, but under grace. But God be thanked, that you were the servants of sin, but you have obeyed from the heart that form of doctrine, which was delivered you. 18 Being then made free from sin, you became the servants of righteousness."

The birth, death and resurrection of Jesus as a man is all about the forgiveness of our sins, taking away our sin nature, and then giving us His nature so that we can now stand in the presence of God whole and complete as if we had never sinned. As stated earlier, how one thinks and what he believes will either promote prosperity or defeat in his life.

Remember there are two kinds of knowledge: (1) natural, as taught in our schools and universities that are limited to our five senses. (2) Spiritual that reveals God is and who He says He is, and what He has done.

Looking to something in the natural will never transform you. If biblical truths are not a reality to you religion will not make it real. Trying to be a Christian will not give you freedom. Being a church member will not make you righteous.

Seven hundred years before Jesus' birth, the prophet Isaiah looked ahead into the corridors of faith and saw God doing something about the plight of man. He recorded what Jesus would be and do for us in Isaiah 53:1-8, "Who has believed our report? And to whom has the arm of the LORD been revealed? For He shall grow up before Him as a tender plant, And as a root out of dry ground. He has no form or comeliness; and when we see Him, There is no beauty that we should desire Him. He is despised and rejected by men, A Man of sorrows and acquainted with grief. And we hid, as it were, our faces from Him; He was despised, and we did not esteem Him. Surely He has borne our grief's And carried our sorrows; Yet we esteemed Him stricken, Smitten by God, and afflicted. But He was wounded for our transgressions, He was bruised for our iniquities; the chastisement for our peace was upon Him, and by His stripes we are healed. All we like sheep have gone astray; we have turned, every one, to his own way; and the LORD has laid on Him the iniquity of us all. He was oppressed and He was afflicted, Yet He opened not His mouth; He was led as a lamb to the slaughter, and as a sheep before its shearers is silent, So He opened not His mouth. He was taken from prison and from judgment, and who will declare His generation? For He was cut off from the land of the living; for the transgressions of My people He was stricken. 9 And they made His grave with the wicked — But with the rich at His death, Because He had done no violence, nor was any deceit in His mouth. Yet it pleased the LORD to bruise Him; He has put Him to grief. When You make His soul an offering for sin, He shall see His seed, He shall prolong His days, And the pleasure of the LORD shall prosper in His hand. He shall see the labor of His soul, and be satisfied. By His knowledge My righteous Servant shall justify many, For He shall bear their iniquities. Therefore I will divide Him a portion with the great, And He shall divide the spoil with the strong, Because He poured out His soul unto death, And He was numbered with the transgressors, And He bore the sin of many, And made intercession for the transgressors."

Isaiah states ten awesome things Jesus did for us:

1. Bore our grief's (sickness, weakness, distress), v. 4.
2. Carried our sorrows (pain), v. 4.
3. Was wounded for our transgressions, v.5.
4. Was bruised for our iniquities (guilt), v. 5.
5. Was chastised (needful to obtain peace and well being for us), v. 5.
6. Healed us (made us whole) through His stripes (that wounded Him), v. 5.
7. Had laid on Him the iniquity of us all, v. 6.
8. He was stricken (to his death) for our transgressions, v.8.

9. He bore our iniquities (in so doing he makes many righteous), v.11.
10. He bore (and took away) the sin of many, v.12.

There is no way to overemphasize the significance of what Jesus did for us. The Apostle Peter explained it this way in 1 Peter 1:3, "Blessed *be* the God and Father of our Lord Jesus Christ, who according to His abundant mercy has begotten us again to a living hope through the resurrection of Jesus Christ from the dead, to an inheritance incorruptible and undefiled and that does not fade away, reserved in heaven for you, who are kept by the power of God through faith for salvation ready to be revealed in the last time."

Peter said we have been begotten again to a living hope. Begotten means to produce again, be born again, born anew and to have one's mind changed so that he lives a new life conformed to the will of God. It is rendered from the meaning of twice and is used chiefly in two senses, with reference to repeated action and rhetorically, in the sense of "moreover" or "further," indicating a statement to be made in the course of an argument or with the meaning "on the other hand." The premise being brought to us is that the Resurrection of Jesus is God doing again something to change one's mind. In this case it is with regard to salvation or being reunited with God.

We have seen that in the Garden of Eden when Adam and Eve sinned it allowed Satan to take control of earth. And God declared that he would bring forth the seed of woman to take back the authority given to Satan. To take this a step further, what you see happening in the world today is a result of Satan becoming the god of this world and using the authority of Adam for evil whereas God desired for Adam to use it as a blessing. Thus we find Jesus, as the second Adam, did what God intended for the first Adam to do.

For some, Jesus is all about Christmas Eve church service to celebrate the beginning of Jesus' life. It is seen as an opportunity to give and receive gifts and go to parties.

Some think Easter is all about celebrating Jesus death and resurrection. Many see Easter as a time for buying new clothes, or the receiving gifts from the Easter bunny and egg hunting.

But Christmas is not the beginning of Jesus' life nor is Easter the climax of his life. Jesus is God and has always existed. Therefore the manger is not more important than the cross He died upon. Nor is the cross more important than the resurrection. Nor is the resurrection more important than His present day ministry. Nor is His present day ministry more important than the conclusion, when He delivers all back to God.

Christmas is about God becoming a man and providing a means for us to be delivered from this world and go beyond Adam to becoming His sons as revealed in Hebrews 2:10, "For it became him, for whom (are) all things, and by whom (are) all things, in bringing many sons unto glory, to make the captain of their salvation perfect through sufferings." Jesus, through His death and resurrection, was the first of many sons according to Romans 8:29, "For whom he did foreknow, he also did predestinate (to be) conformed to the image of his Son, that he might be the firstborn among many brethren."

We saw in the last chapter that Satan established his kingdom and released all type of evil activity. This demonstrated that man could not rule over Satan or overcome sin regardless of what he tried. When man had exhausted every possibility he became helpless with no way to escape and then God provided a way—Jesus (Romans 5:6).

In becoming a natural man, Jesus accomplished three vital objectives. (1) He demonstrated God's process was and is for our good. (2) All of creation was corrupt and had to be done away with, and since all of creation is in and of Jesus, his death put all of creation to death. (3) His resurrection brought forth a new heaven, earth, and a new man.

In the next chapter we will see that the present day ministry of the resurrected Jesus is greater than His minstry on earth as a natural man.

SEVEN

Jesus Our High Priest

Jesus, as a man on earth, operated as a prophet. He began closing this time of prophetic ministry prophesying about the destruction of the Temple in Jerusalem and future events, including His betrayal, death, burial, resurrection and return (Matthew 24 and 25; Mark 13; Luke 21).

We have seen the reality that Jesus still lives today, but what is He doing? His resurrection began a new and more excellent ministry as High Priest, intercessor, and Mediator of a better covenant. When Jesus returns, He will enter into His kingly ministry and will complete His duties of prophet, priest, and king. Lastly, when he has put down all rule, authority and power, having put all his enemies under his feet, the last one being death, he will turn everything back to the Father (Hebrews 4:14; Hebrews 7:25; 1 Corinthians 15:24-26).

When Jesus was ministering on earth as a natural man Judaism was the only religion God had ordained to worship Him. All religions offer some means of worship; a man, a ritual, or whatever, that is suppose to give you spirituality. As we have learned, Christianity is not another religion but an intimate personal relationship with God through Jesus.

The book of Hebrews, however, reveals that Judaism was symbolic of heavenly attributes and a new thing God did and is doing through Jesus. It has two main sections; the first is a doctrinal study of the Son of God, the mediator of a better covenant and secondly a practical application of applying the power of salvation in our lives. We will first examine the doctrinal side, as a proper understanding of it will assist in explaining the practical.

God instructed Moses in Exodus 25 to make Him a sanctuary and gave specific details for its construction. Hebrews chapter nine states that this Temple (tent) used in the Jewish worship was a natural, man made type of the one in heaven. It was enclosed within a wall that had only one entrance point signifying there was only one way to enter. Spiritually it relates to Jesus declaring He is the doorway and only way to God (John 10).

When one entered the temple he would see an altar, where various sacrifices for sins and thanksgiving were offered to God (equal to the Christian cross). Behind the altar was a basin filled with water for washings (think of baptism). Next was a tent that only the priest could enter. It had two compartments. In the outer compartment, called the Holy Place, were a lamp stand and a table with loaves of bread. (In the New Testament Jesus declared he was the light of the world and the bread of life, John 6:35; 10:7).

A veil separated the Holy Place from the second compartment, called the Holy of Holies. It had the Ark or Chest of the Covenant. Inside the ark was a jar holding a sample of the bread (manna) God sent from heaven to feed the Israelites, the rod of Aaron that sprouted, and two stone slabs bearing the Ten Commandments God gave Moses. Above the ark was the Mercy Seat with two representations of the cherubim, (winged creatures symbolic of glory), whose wings touched.

There was also a golden altar for burning incense, which was placed outside the veil in order for the priest to perform the daily ritual because only the high priest could enter once a year, into the second compartment. When the High Priest entered the Holy of Holies he was required to take sacrifice of blood, which he offered for himself and the sins of the people.

This tells us that the way into the Holy of Holies was not yet available since it would require a perfect priest (not a man from Adam) and pure blood (not of an animal), as life is in the blood. Thus all the various rituals acts of worship used in this religion could not cleanse the conscience of guilt and were only in place until God's plan of redemption, a new covenant and a new priesthood, were accomplished.

Therefore when Jesus was resurrected He became the High Priest and entered into the true Holy of Holies in heaven with His own blood that secured a complete and forever forgiveness of our sins. In so doing God established a new covenant and a new priesthood that was superior to the Jewish religion

Hebrews 4:14-16; 5:6, explains what Jesus priestly ministry means for us today: "Seeing then that we have a great High Priest who has passed through the heavens, Jesus the Son of God, let us hold fast our confession. For we do not have a High Priest who cannot sympathize with our weaknesses, but was in all points tempted as we are, yet without sin. Let us therefore come boldly to the throne of grace that we may obtain mercy and find grace to help in time of need. For every high priest taken from among men is appointed for men in things pertaining to God, that he may offer both gifts and sacrifices for sins. He can have compassion on those who are ignorant and going astray, since he himself is also subject to weakness. Because of this he is required as for the people, so also for himself, to offer sacrifices for sins. And no man takes this honor to himself, but he who is called by God, just as Aaron was. So also Christ did not glorify Himself to become High Priest, but it was He who said to Him: "You are My Son, Today I have begotten You." As He also says in another place: "You are a priest forever According to the order of Melchizedek".

In verse 14 we read *having a great High Priest,* referring to what was said about Jesus in chapter two. The force of this verse is in the word *have* for there is nothing that touches us like the sense of ownership. I have a car. I have a house. I have a new dress.

Here we learn that when you come to Jesus you now have a great high priest, *who has* already *ascended and passed through the heavens.* Religions are trying to find a way to heaven and Jesus has already passed through the heavens.

Verse 14 also mentions Jesus' humanity and divinity, *Jesus the Son of God.* It is one thing for God to know our weaknesses and inabilities because he is omnipotent (all knowing). In Hebrews we discover He knows from personal experience what it is like to be a human being. In his humanity we see that Jesus overcame the devil, sin and the world. From this personal experience he knows exactly what it is like to be hungry, tired, and to deal with the mind and emotions as they try to rule our lives.

We are told when Jesus was facing the circumstances of being human he prayed with strong tears. God heard him because he had reverence and respect for His divine authority. Likewise He can be touched when we cry out to Him as revealed in Isaiah 63:9, "In all their affliction he was afflicted, and the angel of his presence saved them: in his love and in his pity he redeemed them; and he bare them, and carried them all the days of old."

A priest loves people and hurts when they hurt, therefore he reaches out in love to encourage and comfort them. The devil knows this and tries every way possible to keep us from the truth that Jesus is now our High Priest.

We are commanded in verse sixteen, "Let us then fearless and confidently and boldly draw near to the throne of grace—the throne of God's unmerited favor (to us sinners); that we may receive mercy (for our failures) and find grace to help in time for every need—appropriate help and well-timed help, coming just when we need it." Not one single feeble person should be afraid to draw near to God, or in drawing near, or doubt, as to whether He really understands or cares. Nor should there be any fear that He will reject you or condemn your weakness.

The Holy Spirit also uses Jesus' example of praying to demonstrate that prayer is drawing near to God. Prayer at first is usually done with fear and trembling. First, we dare talk to God, whom we know is running the universe and having to deal with some really big problems. Then to our amazement we discover He wasn't too busy after all, and our little problem was not interfering with all those big problems. He really listens and hears. We also learn He knows and understands us even better than we know ourselves. It is in prayer we begin to unearth His mercy, compassion, love, and forgiveness. We learn He does not reject us but on the contrary pardons and accepts us.

It is through the prayer process that His grace and the desire to do His will is imparted to us and enables us to go from faith to faith, strength to strength and glory to gory. Each time we pray our confidence (boldness) is increasing and eliminating fear and doubt, and assuring us He loves us. In so doing we become a child who truly loves and trusts his father.

Hebrews 5:1-6 reveals the priesthood was to act in behalf of man to God. Therefore Jesus became a man who can empathize with our weaknesses and ignorance and deals gently with us rather than being critical and judgmental.

When you make the decision to live to please God rather than self you discover how selfish you really are and continually fall short of your vows, even in areas that seem so little and easy. I know this was true for me. I thought I was basically a good person with a few problems but the more I tried to be a Christian the more I messed up. When an Evangelist came to hold a series of meetings in our church it seemed I was facing every wrong thing he talked about. I knew after a few nights of listening to him that I had never gotten saved. So I told him about giving my heart to Jesus but now I was not sure I got saved.

He said, "Let me ask you a few questions. Before you had this experience with Jesus did you ever read your Bible?"

"Oh no sir, I read Sports Illustrated but not the Bible," I replied.

He then asked, "how about now, do you ever read your Bible?"

"Yes sir. I read it all the time", was my answer.

Then he asked, "Before you had this experience with Jesus did you ever pray?"

I answered, "No sir."

"How about now, do you ever pray" he asked?

"Yes sir, I try to pray in the morning and at bed time," was my answer.

"Before you had this experience with Jesus did you ever talk to anyone about Jesus", was his next question?

I replied that I never did talk about Jesus. "How about now", he asked?

I told him I was constantly talking about Jesus. He looked me right in the eye and asked, "So what's your problem?"

Suddenly all the fear of not being saved was gone and I've been saved ever since.

Did you know that when you gave your life to Jesus to rule over you that you became a priest as revealed in Revelation 1: 6, "And has made us kings and priests unto God and his Father; to him be glory and dominion for ever and ever. Amen?"

Jesus demonstrates that the true character and nature of priesthood is rooted in sonship. He left His high position of glory and became one of us. He yielded His will and His life to make it possible for us to once again experience the joy of knowing God. Now God looks to you and me to be His Sons and daughters, expecting us to act as his priest and show forth His glory on planet earth.

At the root of priestly ministry is a sense of oneness and identity with the weakness of yourself and others that results in crying out to God for help. Because we do not always act like a priest in our personal relationships Jesus is sometimes not revealed. Instead others see our selfishness or religiosity.

When I started to work in the chemical industry I never dealt gently or had sympathy for others, nor would I overlook their mistakes. In fact, if an employee did not act or do as I thought they should I would get mad and speak harshly. When God began to deal with me about this attitude I put up this sign in my office to remind me to be gentle with others; "I can understand my mistakes because I'm only human. It is your dumb inexcusable ones that upset me."

Furthermore we learn from Hebrews that no man can take the honor of priesthood unto himself—he must be called of God. This truth is vey important to Christianity. Every religion has a founder who claimed to be sent from God or who had a mystic call to lead people into eternal bliss such as Mohammed, Buddha, and others. The founder recited things that are written in a book. When the founder dies his followers try to do what it says. Muslims, for example, have their doctrines of the Quran. They only have four schools of interpretation. Whereas Christianity has hundreds—Calvinist, Armenians, Protestants, Catholics, pre, post and mid millennium—who fuss and throw Scriptures at each other as though Christ is dead just like Mohammed.

Furthermore, most churches seldom talk about Jesus' present day ministry but about what He did 2000 years ago. They talk about Him feeding 5000 or walking on water or cursing a fig tree or raising the dead. It is as though His ministry ended 2000 years ago.

I write this next statement with sadness of heart. A new convert learns in about six months the essential facts about Jesus—forgiveness of sin, the trinity, second coming, Easter, and Christmas. They quickly learn their spiritual growth is measured by how much money they contribute, how many meetings they attend, and involvement in church programs. Due to "business" there is no time to develop meaningful relationships and they learn that activity has not produce the spiritual growth they desired. Before long they are burned out with no sense of God's call, purpose, and plans for their lives. Slowly but surely they withdraw from church activity and may even leave the church.

This almost happened to me as I became bored with "playing church". I began thinking there had to be more to being saved than just going to meetings and trying to be a Christian. This in turn led me to a whole new relationship with God as we shall see in the next chapter.

THIRD D

EIGHT

The Holy Spirit

The Holy Spirit is not an impersonal force but the third person of the Godhead with attributes that are ascribed to God. For example, He is present everywhere (Psalms 139:7-8). He has all wisdom and knowledge (1 Corinthians 2:10). He possesses infinite power (Luke 1:35).

Furthermore we find the Holy Spirit does things that only God can do, such as creating and giving life (Genesis 1:2; Romans 8:11). In addition, he engages us in personal ways. For example he grieves when we sin (Ephesians 4: 29-30) He teaches us spiritual truths (1 Corinthians 2: 13). He prays and intercedes for us (Romans 8:26). He guides us (John 16:13). He gives us spiritual gifts (1 Corinthians 12:11). He convicts of sin, and of righteousness, and of judgment. (John 16:8) He gives us assurance we are saved. (Romans 8:16). He empowers us to overcome sin (Romans 8:2).

One of the ways Jesus prepared the disciples for dealing with his entrance into the High Priestly ministry was to assure them He was not abandoning them. He told them he was not going to leave them as orphans on earth but would send them a Helper and Counselor, the Spirit of truth whom the world could not receive who would teach them all things and bring to remembrance all the things Jesus had said to them (John 14:16-18).

Here we find Jesus is introducing a new work of the Holy Spirit.

In the first covenant, the Holy Spirit did not dwell in the heart of people, but came upon them in various ways and at different times to demonstrate who God was.

The prophets, however, understood the time would come when the Spirit of God would be poured out on all flesh. Ezekiel prophesied the time would come when God's Spirit would dwell in our hearts, "And I will put my spirit within you, and cause you to walk in my statutes, and ye shall keep my judgments, and do *them*" (36:27).

Joel, for example, declared, "And it shall come to pass afterward, *that* I will pour out my spirit upon all flesh; and your sons and your daughters shall prophesy, your old men shall dream dreams, your young men shall see visions: And also upon the servants and upon the handmaids in those days will I pour out my spirit" (28-29)

Jesus further declared this outpouring of the Holy Spirit would take place when he was glorified in John 7:37-39 "On the last day, that great *day* of the feast, Jesus stood and cried out, saying, "If anyone thirsts, let him come to Me and drink. He who believes in Me, as the Scripture has said, out of his heart will flow rivers of living water. But this He spoke concerning the Spirit, whom those believing in Him would receive; for the Holy Spirit was not yet *given*, because Jesus was not yet glorified."

We are told in Acts chapter one and two how this was fulfilled. After Jesus was resurrected he spent forty days teaching His disciples things pertaining to the Kingdom of God, and commanded them to not depart from Jerusalem, but wait for the baptism of the Holy Spirit that God had promised. On the 50th day after the resurrection, called Pentecost, there were about 120 disciples gathered in an upper room praying. Suddenly a sound from heaven, like a rushing mighty wind, filled the whole house in which they were sitting. Then there appeared to them divided tongues, as of fire, and one sat upon each of them. And they were all filled with the Holy Spirit and began to speak with other tongues, as the Spirit gave them utterance (Acts 1:1-5; 13-14; 2:1-5).

As word got out about this event a multitude gathered consisting of people from various countries that were confounded because they heard the disciples speaking in their own language and wondered what it meant. Some were in doubt; others mocked and said they were drunk. But Peter stood up and declared it was not drunkenness but that which had been spoken of by the prophet Joel (Acts 2:6-18)

He further explained what God was doing in Acts 2:36-41 "Therefore let all the house of Israel know assuredly that God has made this Jesus, whom you crucified, both Lord and Christ. Now when they heard this, they were cut to the heart, and said to Peter and the rest of the apostles,"' Men and brethren, what shall we do? "' Then Peter said to them, "'Repent, and let every one of you be baptized in the name of Jesus Christ for the remission of sins; and you shall receive the gift of the Holy Spirit. "For the promise is to you and to your children, and to all who are afar off, as many as the Lord our God will call."' And with many other words he testified and exhorted them, saying, "'Be saved from this perverse generation." Then those who gladly received his word were baptized; and that day about three thousand souls were added to them."

Jesus declared in John 16: 8-11 the Holy Spirit would reprove the world of sin, righteousness and judgment. In verse 37, above we see this being fulfilled when they heard God had made Jesus both Lord and Messiah (Christ) and were pierced in their hearts and wanted to know what to do. Peter gave them three things to do: repent, be baptized, and receive the gift of the Holy Spirit.

True repentance is turning from trying to be your own god to acknowledging Jesus is your Lord and involves an inward change of the mind and an outward change of behavior. You may have heard it said, "Now that Jesus is your Savior you need to make Him your Lord." This is a wrong concept. You cannot make Him Lord—God has already done it. Therefore you can only accept Him as your Lord. If He is not your Lord He cannot be your savior.

Acknowledging the Lordship of Jesus changes your life from one of pleasing self to one of pleasing God. The Lordship of Jesus also involves denying self, taking up your cross, and following him (Matthew 16:24-27).

Denying self is not the same as self-denial, which involves giving up something. Denying self is confronting the root problem of being your own god. Because Jesus is now your Lord, anytime self tries to act independent of God, you deny it that right. In so doing you refuse to let self control your life and allow the Holy Spirit be in control.

The cross Jesus was speaking about occurs when your thinking intersects with the word of God. At this intersection, you deny what you think and *let God's Word be the final authority in your life*. For example, you do not think God does not love you, but the Word says He loves you so you deny the feelings and accept the fact that God loves you.

Also, when your will crosses the will of God you deny self and obey God. You may not want to pray but God commands us to not worry but pray about everything. Therefore you deny self and pray instead of worrying.

Repentance also involves acknowledging you have sinned and asking for God's forgiveness. When you do, God will not only forgive you, He will cleanse you from all unrighteousness (Psalms 32:5-6; 1 John 1:9-10).

We saw that after Adam and Eve sinned they hid from God. We read in Genesis 3:9, "Then the LORD God called to Adam and said to him, 'Where *are* you?' "God's search continues today as revealed in Luke 19:10, "For the Son of Man has come to seek and to save that which was lost." And in John 6:44 Jesus declares, "No one can come to Me unless the Father who sent Me draws him; and I will raise him up at the last day." Here we see love in action. God not only provided a way to forgive our sins, He now pursues us through Jesus. Otherwise, we would stay in sin until we die as so many do.

We have seen that *true repentance brings total forgiveness of your sins*. This is called being born again. Once you are born again there is another spiritual event that is vital to your spiritual growth: water baptism. Peter said after you have repented you are to be water baptized.

Notice that the Lordship of Jesus is required before you can be water baptized. You may have a religious baptismal ceremony, but you cannot be baptized unless you have truly repented. This applies to adults and children—there are no exceptions.

This passage in Acts reveals those who received Peter's message immediately responded with obedience and were baptized. We can also see this same attitude in Acts 8:35-37 when Phillip preached Jesus to an Ethiopian eunuch and the eunuch asked if anything could hinder him from being baptized. Phillip told him he had to believe in Jesus with all his heart. To this, the Eunuch replied that he believed Jesus Christ is the Son of God (Lordship) and Phillip baptized him.

The point I am making is that baptism is more than a ceremony or a spiritual symbolism as seen from these results of being water baptized:

- Burying the old body of sin (Romans 6:4-5).
- A circumcision (to cut all around) without hands to remove the body of sin as we have faith in the operation (Colossians 2:11-12).
- The cleansing of the conscience (1 Peter 3:21).
- Being raised to walk in newness of life (Romans 6:3-5).
- Being added to the church (Acts 2:41b).

The third vital element of Peter's answer was to receive the gifting of the Holy Spirit. It is in the gifting of the Holy Spirit that we run into various misunderstandings and false teaching. At the beginning of the 20th century the prevailing teaching in the church regarding the Holy Spirit was called Cessationism. This view held that the gifting of the Holy Spirit ceased when the last Apostle died in the first century. Then, in 1901 a Holy Spirit revival broke out at a Bible college in Topeka Kansas when Charles E Parham encouraged students at his Bethel Bible School, to pray for the gift of tongues. Along with his students (Agnes Ozman was the first), he was baptized in the Spirit and spoke in tongues in early January.

Three years later a similar move of the Holy Spirit swept over Wales of the United Kingdom, making it the largest Christian revival at that time, and began to spread worldwide.

In 1906, the Holy Spirit fell on a preacher, William Seymour, at a church on Azusa Street in Los Angeles, which birthed the Pentecostal Movement and the ministry of the Holy Spirit became a flood in 1948.

In the 50's Oral Roberts had tent meetings with powerful healings. Billy Graham began to touch lives through evangelistic crusades, and the Charismatic Movement that began in 1960 continues to thrive today.

Scripture reveals these blessings accompany being baptized in the Holy Spirit:

- The power to boldly witness (Acts 1:8),
- Ability to heal the sick (Acts 4:8-12).
- Power to preach, perform miracles, cast out unclean spirits, and baptize others in the Holy Spirit (Acts 8:4-17).
- Ability to see visions (Acts 10:44-46),
- Ability to prophesy (Acts 19:6).
- Receiving spiritual revelation (2 Corinthians 2:10).
- Ability to speak in unlearned languages (Acts 2:4).

There are many special blessings associated with speaking in unlearned languages such as speaking directly to God and speaking mysteries. When you don't know what or how to pray you are no longer limited to only praying with your understanding as you can now pray with the Spirit. In those times you are so blessed that giving thanks by your mind and emotions are not adequate you give thanks well in the spirit. Speaking in tongues also builds up your faith and keep you in the love realm (1 Corinthians 14: 2, 15, 17; Jude 20)

Perhaps my experience will shed some light on being baptized in the Holy Spirit. I sincerely gave my life over to Jesus and was born again spiritually in 1959. I had heard that God was love but only mentally believed it due to all the hurts and rejection I was carrying around in my emotions. I joined a church and became involved in all phases of church activity hoping I could earn God's love. I even went to choir practice a couple of times, even though I could not sing because the music leader (he was a friend) insisted they could teach me to sing. When I was not invited back I ask him why? He said, "most people sing off key and I can help them but you have an unusual talent, you sing in between keys and I can't help you." I can truly say, from my experience, activities will not make you a strong Christian, or I would have become a superman Christian.

It took me 12 years of doing various religious works to realize there was something missing but I had no clue as to what it could be. I talked to my Pastor and he counseled me that maybe God was calling me to preach. I did not tell him what I thought about that idea, but I knew from being on the deacon board that was the last job on earth I would ever want.

So I cried out to God and He told me my problem was never spending time alone with Him and this made me evaluate my routine. It was like this: Get up in the morning. Find just enough time to gulp down a few bites of breakfast. Go to work. Come home. Either rush off to coach or go to a sport activity the boys were involved in, or attend a civic or church meeting. Come home exhausted. Put the boys to bed. Lie down in my bed too tired to pray or read my Bible. Yet I did find time to read the sports page of our local newspaper and the Sports Illustrated magazine.

The only way I could think of to have time alone with God was to set my clock for one hour earlier and get up before the family awoke. That first morning I was not sure what to do and finally decided I should read my Bible. I opened it and began to read. When I awoke I was late for work. On my way to work I realized the mistake I had made. Some people read to go asleep. I should have prayed instead of reading.

The next morning I again got up early. This time I knelt down by the sofa and began to pray. When I awoke I was again late for work. I thought getting up early might be okay for some people, but obviously it was not for me. So I went back to rising at my regular time.

After a few days the Lord again spoke to me with regard to spending time alone with him. I told him I had tried but kept falling asleep and that if I kept being late to work I would be fired. He then asked if I would like a suggestion for a time to be alone with him.

"Sure," I eagerly said.

Then he questioned, "How about your lunch hour?"

I could not believe it. How could a loving caring God be so cruel? Lunch was the time I went out with over guys to eat and talked about sports. I also secretly knew if I did not go to lunch they would want to know why. It was one thing to be a deacon, but quite another to be a crazy Christian who took his lunch hour to be alone with God. But since I had no better plan I said okay.

Looking back I wonder how I could have still been breathing and been that dumb. Think about it, the God of the Universe desires to have time just with me and I am basically replying that I don't see how I can fit you into my schedule.

The next day I used my lunchtime to be alone with God. I sat at my desk and opened my Bible and asked God where to begin. He then asked me a question, "Are you willing to lay aside the teachings and traditions of man and accept what I will teach you?" I said, "Yes."

"Okay, let's start in the book of Acts", was his reply.

It was during these lunchtimes that I saw in Acts it was a common practice for people to repent, be baptized in water and when they were raised up out of the water hands would be laid on them and they would begin to speak in tongues and prophesied (Acts 19:6) The Holy Spirit was revealing to me, I needed to be baptized in the Holy Spirit.

When he showed me in Luke 24:49 that Jesus commanded the disciples to wait in the city of Jerusalem until they were endued with power from on high He asked me, "Do you think it should be any different for you"?

I told Him, "No, it would be the same."

He then reminded me that after I acknowledged Jesus as my Lord I joined a church and immediately went to work without waiting to be endued with power from on high. I immediately knew he was referring to the power from on high that comes through being baptized in the Holy Spirit (Acts 1:8).

I repented for not waiting and asked Jesus to baptize me in the Holy Spirit, and secretly wondered how the Holy Spirit was going to speak in tongues (I had seen in Acts 2 that they began to speak in tongues as the Spirit gave utterance). To my surprise nothing happened after I prayed. No fire came, no wind rushed in, and no tongues escaped my lips. I was devastated. Then I thought that having my mouth closed had stopped the Holy Spirit from speaking. So I opened my mouth and still nothing happened and I became very confused. Then the accusation began to creep in. God did not love me as He did them or I must have sin in my life.

It took me awhile to get over this discouraging experience and realize that somehow I had missed something in the Acts account. I began seeking God for the answer and did not get a response. This upset me even more as I was sincerely willing to do whatever He said.

A few weeks later a friend asked me to attend a church meeting with him in a near by city. As I listened to the speaker it dawned on me he could speak with power and authority because he was filled with the Holy Spirit. Suddenly I had the answer to what I had missed. In Acts the disciples laid hands on people to receive the baptism of the Holy Spirit, but no one had laid hands on me.

I devised a plan to have him lay hands on me so I could receive the Holy Spirit. My plan was to wait until no one was around him after the service and ask if he knew anything about being baptized in the Holy Spirit. When the time was right I approached him and asked my question. Suddenly my friend popped up from behind the podium and told him I had been seeking the baptism for several weeks.

"Is that right", he asked?

I told him how I had prayed and nothing happened.

Then he asked me if I was familiar with Luke chapter eleven. I said, "No," and he opened his Bible and read verses nine through thirteen; "So I say to you, ask, and it will be given to you; seek, and you will find; knock, and it will be opened to you. For everyone who asks receives, and he who seeks finds, and to him who knocks it will be opened. If a son asks for bread from any father among you, will he give him a stone? Or if *he asks* for a fish, will he give him a serpent instead of a fish? Or if he asks for an egg, will he offer him a scorpion? If you then, being evil, know how to give good gifts to your children, how much more will *your* heavenly Father give the Holy Spirit to those who ask Him!"

"Do you realize that you called God a liar just now?" he asked?

I was so shocked I waited a moment before asking why he would say that. He proceeded to tell me that I said when I asked to be baptized in the Holy Spirit nothing happened.

"But if I did not receive tongues after I prayed how could I be calling God a liar," I asked?

He answered, "There is nothing in these verses about tongues." Then he asked me if I thought God would lie?

I said, "No."

"Well," he said, "we just read that if you asked for the gift of the Holy Spirit God would give you the gift. So when you asked, God either gave you the gift or he lied."

I asked, "What about tongues"?

"You'll never speak in tongues until you first believe you have received," was his reply, "so don't worry about it, you'll soon be speaking in tongues. It's like buying a pair of shoes, tongues comes with them, and tongues come with the Holy Spirit. But tongues is just one of the many blessings that result in receiving the Holy Spirit."

This completely freed me as I realized my mistake was thinking I had to speak in tongues to receive the Holy Spirit instead of receiving by faith in the word of God. It was a wonderful relief to be over the war of speaking in tongues.

During this time in my life it took me about twenty minutes to drive to work and I usually spent that time praying, worshipping, singing and praising the Lord. Then it happened; one morning as I was singing I found myself using words that were not English. However it did not dawn on me what I had done until the next day. That morning as I sat in my office a preacher, who worked in the maintenance department, came into the office and dropped a booklet on my desk and said the Holy Spirit had impressed him I needed to see that booklet.

After he left I opened the booklet and saw it was about people being baptized in the Holy Spirit. I thought it was strange since that issue was all settled. Then I thought that if the Lord had instructed him to give me the booklet, I needed to at least ask the Holy Spirit to show me what to read. I began to turn the pages. When the Holy Spirit instructed me to stop I read a testimony of a woman receiving and singing in the spirit rather than speaking in tongues.

Immediately the Holy Spirit spoke that this was what had happened to me. I was dumbfounded, because I was not aware that I had sung in the spirit. How could this apply to me? The Holy Spirit reminded me of my singing in English and then using words that were not English yesterday morning.

Wow! I was so thrilled I almost shouted. I remembered the Apostle Paul had told the Corinthians that he prayed in the spirit and with the understanding and that he sang in the spirit and with understanding (1 Corinthians 14:15).

This caused me to think that since I was singing in the spirit I could also pray in the spirit. I could hardly wait to get home and do so. At home I knelt down by the couch and thanked the Lord for the blessing. Then I started speaking in tongues.

In a few moments I heard the suggestion I was not speaking in spiritual tongues but just jabbering a bunch of gibberish. I listened to myself, and my utterance did sound like awful nonsense.

Then I heard a suggestion the Holy Spirit was not speaking through me, and that I was making up the words. This really got my attention and I did something that would change my life forever. I stopped speaking and asked the Lord, "How do I know if it is the Holy Spirit or just me making up sounds?" I heard a voice that was so audible I did not know if it came from the inside of me or if Jesus was standing right next to me so I was afraid to open my eyes as I heard, " it is by faith." I then said out loud, "Get out of here devil you are not going to steal this blessing from me." I've been speaking in tongues ever since.

After awhile my office became an awesome place where I met God on a daily basis and He became real to me. I went from trying to worship and having faith in concepts of a God who lived up yonder somewhere to an intimacy with the God who lives in my heart.

However I had no idea God was after something far greater than getting my spiritual life on tract. It wasn't too long after I spoke in tongues that a friend invited me to attend a Campus Crusade For Christ conference.

At this conference one of the sessions was on a cleansed life. The bottom line was that to be useful to God one must be a pure vessel. At the end of the teaching we were told to take thirty minutes, go to our room and ask the Holy Spirit to show us any area in our life that needed to be purified and to reveal any sin we had not repented of.

I thought this did not apply to me as I had developed the habit of always asking the Lord to forgive me of my sins. Once in my room I decided to obey the instruction to get it over with and then figure out how I would spend the rest of the time.

When I asked the Holy Spirit to reveal any sin I needed to confess He brought up something that went back a few years. I was so shocked at first I did not know how to respond and then said, "But I know I have asked for my sins to be forgiven since that occurred."

The Holy Spirit replied, "I've had a problem with you doing that as I never knew exactly which sin you were repenting of. My Word tells you to confess your sin and receive forgiveness but you have never confessed a sin to Me. Would you like to confess this sin and be forgiven."

I sat there stunned as this truth hit me like a ton of bricks falling on my head. I thought how foolish I had been and compared it to grocery shopping. You don't shop for "groceries" but for specific items on your grocery list.

Soon I had a sin list with specific items to repent of and receive forgiveness. I opened my Bible to 1 John 1:9, "If we confess our sins, He is faithful and just to forgive us our sins and to cleanse us from all unrighteousness." I destroyed the sin list as all those sins had been confessed and I had been forgiven.

Another life changing seminar at this conference taught on a total surrender of your life in every area to God. The speaker used an illustrating to make his point: The father of a young boy was away from home for a long time. When he returned his son ran to meet him and said, "Daddy I have missed you and want to show you how much I love you. I have decided to give my life to you to do with as you please."

"Le me get this straight, you are telling me I can now do anything with your life I want to do," asked the father?

"Yes, yes the son answered," all excited about his decision.

"Okay, this is what I am going to do, I am going to take away all your toys and then lock you in your room. When I call you come running to eat the spinach I will feed you daily," said the father.

There was a mixed reaction from the students. Some were silent and some nervously laughed, and all felt a little uncomfortable. The instructor explained we felt uncomfortable because we knew this was not a normal reaction.

He then made this observation, we somehow get the idea that if we told God I want to show you how much I love you by giving you my life to do anything with you so desire He would take away all our toys and make us miserable. The truth is just the opposite. I have never heard anyone testify they gave their life to God and He made them so miserable they wish they had never done it. But I have heard many testify they gave their life to God and He made life worth living and they wish they had done it sooner.

I began to weep as the Holy Spirit told me I had never surrendered sports, career, my wife and children or my life to God to do with as He pleased. I silently prayed and told God I wanted to show Him how much I loved Him and from that moment on He could take my life and all my possessions and use me any way He desired. That I would go and do whatever He desired.

As I look back on my life I realize this was a defining moment for me. I returned home a different person and I was astonished to find the Bible made a lot of sense. The Holy Spirit was now teaching me and Scriptures were so exciting I could not read and study the Bible enough. Perhaps it was because I started teaching a Sunday school class right after I got saved and never stopped the Holy Spirit was able to quickly give me revelation of spiritual truths that were life changing.

In my job as Supervisor of a chemical production area the Holy Spirit began to direct me to various ways to improve the efficiency in areas that were performing below standard.

One miracle that still amazes me involved a huge tank of phenol. This chemical had to be kept at a specific temperature range by using hot weater. If it became to warm it would become a dark color and be unusable. If the temperature was too low it would solidify. One day the tank temperature dropped too low and before it was corrected the whole tank was one big solid mass and we could not pump phenol to the production area. This was a major crisis and an emergency meeting was called to bring together key personnel to propose a solution.

It was decided the best way to thaw out the tank would be to make a stainless steel coil and attach a live steam source. The coil would be placed on top of the mass and melt an opening to the bottom of the tank where the pump was located. Then we would circulate the thawed phenol until the tank was completely thawed. Meanwhile we had to pay a premium price to truck in phenol.

Three days later during my lunch hour with the Lord He spoke to me to lay my hands on the phenol tank and pray for it to be thawed out and He would thaw it out.

My first reaction was to ask Him why He would do this. He answered, "Because I love you."

That was good enough for me and I went out to the phenol tank, looked around to see if anyone was watching, and saw no one. I laid my hands on the tank and asked the Lord to thaw it out.

I hurried over to the production area and asked the operator when was the last time he tried to pump phenol. "Just a few minutes ago," he answered, "and its still frozen solid."

I proceeded to tell him the tank was now thawed and we were going to pump over some phenol. He gave me a strange look and followed me over to the tank. We walked up the long stair to the top of the tank and he began to open the valves on the line to the production area.

I placed my hand on one of the pipes to see how hot it was. My heart sank to the pit of my stomach as the pipe was ice cold. I began to panic and feel nauseated.

Suddenly I remembered there was a Scripture that said you built up your faith by praying in tongues (Jude 20). I began to silently pray in my prayer language.

"Okay, I'm all set, do you want me to start the pump", he asked?

"Hit the start button," I replied.

When he did I immediately felt warmth and thought about Elijah praying for rain and sent his servant to see if there were any clouds. On the seventh time he reported there was a cloud about the size of a hand. Elijah responded they needed to hurry down Mount Carmel as there was an abundance of rain coming (1 King 18:41-45).

I said to the operator, "let's hurry over to the building as I hear an abundance of phenol rushing through the pipe." When we arrived at the building phenol was pouring into weigh tank and I asked the operator if this was good flow of phenol and he said it was.

As I turned to leave I said, "Okay, that's good enough for me. See you latter."

"Wait a minute Joe, can I ask you a personal question?"

"Sure, what is it?"

"Where you praying for the tank to be thawed out" he asked?

I replied, "I sure was and God answered my prayer."

"Boy, did He," he replied.

I did not know it but word quickly spread all over the plant that I had prayed and God thawed out the phenol tank.

A few days latter my sectary told me my boss wanted to see me in his office right away. I knew he had been touring the production areas and thought he had found something wrong.

I entered his office and he did not appear to be too happy. "I've been out in the plant and heard some of the operators talking and have a question for you," he said. "Is it true you prayed for the tank to be thawed out and God thawed it out?"

Because he did not seem excited about what he heard I was not sure how to answer him. I thought about it for a few moments and said, "Yes sir, that's what happened."

"Well, why did you wait three days to pray," was his reply.

Soon after this a maintenance worker came to my office and said his Pastor asked him to see if I would be willing to hold a youth revival in their church.

My mind went bonkers and filled with questions over this strange and weird question. Who was this man? Who was his Pastor? Why would his Pastor be asking me to hold a youth revival? I was not a preacher and he did not even know me.

He told me the name of his church and Pastor and said they had invited an evangelist from California to preach the revival and had received a letter he could not come. The Pastor then said, "How about that fellow where you work that you've been telling me about, why don't you ask him and see if he will do it?"

I thought this was so strange it had to be God and since I had told Him He could do anything with my life he desired I said yes.

This started me out in youth evangelism and eventually God raised me up to be Vice President of an international college ministry and sent me to preach and teach all over the world. I say this to attest that God's plan for your life will be revealed as you obey and draw near to Him

God also challenged me in other ways. For example, I had never paid attention to the Scriptures in Mark chapter sixteen that believers could not only speak in new tongues they could lay hands on the sick and they would be healed until one day during my lunch as I read this passage the Holy Spirit asked me what I thought about it. Somehow I knew that if I said I believed he would ask me why I was not laying hands on the sick and seeing them healed.

Since I had never seen a healing or miracle in our church services I was not about to be the first one to suggest we lay hands on the sick. So I replied there were some things in the Bible that were hard to understand.

He responded, "I did not ask if you understood but if you believed?"

Then he asked me if I knew and understood everything about chemistry?

I had to be honest and admit there were many things I did not know or understand about chemistry.

He then asked, "What do you do when you have an issue to come up in the plant that you are not sure what to do?"

"I get one of my chemistry books an look up what it teaches on the subject," I answered.

"Do you always understand what you read in your chemistry book", he asked? Again I had to be honest and say there were times I did not understand what I had read.

"So what do you do?"

"I go talk to Dr. Wood (the chief chemist)."

"Why?"

"Because he has a doctorate in chemistry and knows more than me."

"Do you always understand what he tells you?"

"Not always."

"What do you do if you don't understand him, do you take his word or not?"

Now the pressure was beginning to build as I could see where this was going and I was not too happy about it. In fact I got a little irritated and said, "Sometimes we check it out in the lab to see if it works before we do it in the plant. So I am going to check out your word and if it does not work I am going to forget you and the Bible."

"Go ahead," he said, "try my word out I'm not afraid it will not work."

Looking back on that incident I am so thankful my Dad, and priest, is so kind and gentle. If my son talked that way to me I would not have been so easy on him.

Soon after this I was invited to preach a Sunday morning service at near by church. It went so well they decided to have an evening service if I would come back and preach again. I told them I would and prayed a dismissal prayer.

In our church when the Pastor dismissed us he would go to the entrance door and greet attendees as they left. Since that was how I thought it should be done I quickly went to the entrance door and started greeting people as they left.

When I reached out to shake hands with a little old lady she drew back and I asked her what was the problem? She explained that she was pouring boiling water into a bowl of Jell-O mix to have for lunch and the water splashed out and burned her hand. She held her hand out and it was all red.

I heard a voice on the inside of me say, "Go ahead." "Go ahead what," I asked, but knew exactly what He meant.

"Pray for her, you said you were going to try out my word," was His response.

I had never done anything like that and was not about to get started. Quickly my devious little mind figured a way out. I knew she did not believe in healing so I said, "Ma'am, do you believe God can heal your hand?"

I almost fainted when she said, "I sure do, do you want to pray for it?"

I did not say what I was thinking: "why was she even in church with a scalded hand? People stay home for fewer reasons than that." I knew I was trapped so I held out a hand and asked her to place her hand on top of mine, closed my eyes and prayed, "Lord Jesus I ask you to heal this hand." I could hardly wait to see what had happened. But when I opened my eyes the hand still looked red and scaled. I heard my voice saying, "Ma'am, if you will only believe you will see the healing manifested." That has to be God, I thought, because I don't even believe that.

As I entered the sanctuary that evening I saw her down front with some other ladies. She saw me and came running up holding out her hand and said, "look it is all healed!" I could hardly believe my eyes as her hand looked as though it had never been burned. This made a believer out of me and since then I've seen all types of healings and miracles in my services.

Looking back on my experience I now understand that you cannot give to others something you do not have. The churches I attended in my early years gave me what they had which was salvation. They could not teach and impart signs, wonders, healings and miracles or baptism in the Holy Spirit because they had never experienced it. On the other hand it is disappointing to find churches that claim to be Spirit filled with members not baptized in the Holy Spirit and who do not allow the giftings of the Holy Spirit to operate in their services.

Due to the importance of the present day ministry of the Holy Spirit I am going to review the principle for receiving the Holy Spirit from Luke 11:9-13 "If ye then, being evil, know how to give good gifts unto your children: *how much more shall your heavenly Father give the Holy Spirit to them that ask him?"* (emphasis added). From this we learn receiving the gift of the Holy Spirit is not complicated. It requires asking the Father and trusting in His word that He will do as you have asked. If you have never asked, or, if like me, you asked amiss then pray and ask the Father to baptize you in the Holy Spirit. After asking and receiving, thank Him for the gift. Now lift your hands and begin to worship and praise Him in your new tongue.

NINE

Gifts of the Holy Spirit

The nine major gifts of the Holy Spirit are listed in 1 Corinthians 12 and we are told the administration and operation of them are diverse, but it is the same Spirit at work behind them all for everyone's benefit. For example, if you are in a test or trial and need to understand what is going on, it is good to have someone who has the gift of the word of knowledge and wisdom to pray with you and see what God reveals.

The nine giftings are easily combined into three groups of three:

- Revelatory gifts: wisdom, knowledge, and discerning of spirits.
- Power gifts: faith, healings, and working of miracles.
- Inspirational gifts: prophecy, tongues, and interpretation of tongues.

The word of wisdom is God's revelation of how to deal soundly with conditions and situations. It concerns people, places, or things in the future as to what God will have them do or what He will do. It pertains to things unknown by natural knowledge.

The word of knowledge reveals the mind of God concerning facts in the present and past but not in the future. It is not known facts but revelation understanding.

The gift of faith is not the same as the fruit of faith. Nor is it the measure of faith, which every Christian has been given. This faith is used of God to bring things to pass without any human effort. It is a supernatural knowing and assurance that even though it seems impossible in the natural the event is going to happen, and it does.

Gifts of healing are for the curing of sickness, disease, physical infirmities, and such without natural means or human help. Notice that it states gifts not the singular gift. This is due to the Holy Spirit giving specific faith to those with this ministry to know they have the anointing to heal certain needs, such as sight being restored to blind people, but they do not have this same faith for every need.

Furthermore I find there are different ways healing is administered: there may be an immediate healing, faith healing, and medical healing. Faith healing is being assured that by some act of faith you will be healed. Such as when the woman touched the hem of Jesus garment and was healed (Mark 5:25-34).

Faith healing involves an inward sense that although the healing was not immediately manifested you were healed. For example, when praying for people having to wear glasses and their 20/20 sight is not immediate restored, I instruct them that releasing their faith to be healed is similar to cutting down a tree. Although the tree is cut off from its roots the leaves will stay green for a few days before they turn brown and wither away. So continue to believe and don't wear your glasses unless you must to keep from doing harm, and your eyesight will be restored in due time. Many people did this and now have 20/20 vision.

It so happened, however, as I got older, I began to find my arms were not long enough to hold a book where I could read it. I bought some reading glasses and began using them. One morning during my devotion, as I was reading my Bible, the Lord asked me why I was not practicing what I preached? I asked Him what He meant. He said you've told others to not use their glasses unless it was necessary and here you are using your glasses. I immediately asked for forgiveness, took off the glasses and was able to read clearly for a few minutes. When the print became fuzzy I put the glasses back on. I continued doing this until my 20/20 eyesight was restored.

The working miracles are God using a person, or animal, or some other natural instrument to do something not normally done. This is different than faith that does not involve the use of a person or anything in the natural. They are, however, only miracles to man, as there is nothing impossible with God.

There are many miracles recorded in the Bible and some doubt they occurred, such as Moses dividing the Red Sea (Exodus 14:21) or Balaam's' donkey speaking to him that he should not strike him as he was keeping the angel from killing him (Numbers 21:21-27).

Those who operate in the gift of prophecy are limited to an inspired message to build up, to exhort and to comfort (1 Corinthians 13:3).

The gift of prophecy is not the same as a prophet's ministry and this has created misunderstandings in the church. This difference has been further complicated when a church only has a Pastor and no prophets to judge if the prophesy is a word from God. Many Pastors are so uncomfortable doing this they do not allow this ministry of the Holy Spirit to function (1 Corinthians 14:29). If someone who has the gift of prophecy goes beyond the limitations expressed in 1 Corinthian 13 they are acting as a prophet but do not have the anointing and authority of a prophet. In so doing they are subject to error and if not properly judged can cause harm to others.

A prophet is a gift from Jesus to the church (Ephesians 4:11), The gift of prophecy is a gift from the Holy Spirit. Prophets do not have the limitations of prophesy and may give warnings, directions, guidance, callings, and vision primarily through the gifting of Wisdom, Word of Knowledge, and Discerning of Spirits.

The Discerning of Spirits is insight into the spirit world with regards to good and evil spirits. In the natural realm it involves spirits associated with human activity.

The gift of tongues empowers you to speak in a language you have not learned to bring a message to the assembly. It is different than praying in tongues that is for personal benefit and must be interpreted, preferably by the speaker. If there is no one with the gift of interpretation a message in tongues is not to be given (1 Corinthians 14:27-28).

The interpretation of tongues is not a translation of what has been spoken since a translation is word for word. An interpretation is the meaning of what has been spoken.

From this study you may have found some gifts that interest you, and you would like to operate in them. Great! Ask the Holy Spirit for the gift you desire. Then when the opportunity comes, step out in faith and let the Holy Spirit use your gifting.

TEN

The Fruit of the Holy Spirit

The gifts of the Holy Spirit reveal the power of God while the fruit of the Holy Spirit reveal God's character. The nine fruit of the Spirit is listed in Galatians 5: 22-23, "But the fruit of the Spirit is love, joy, peace, longsuffering, kindness, goodness, faithfulness, gentleness, self-control. Against such there is no law."

When I read there was no law against the fruit of the Holy Spirit I became very excited. I knew from my science studies that a law is absolute and governs conduct and/or action. I also knew that a higher law would supersede a lesser law. Therefore I knew that if I could develop the fruit of the Spirit in my life I would be operating in the highest law in the universe. WOW!

Take the law of gravity as an example of this principle. We usually simplify this law by saying, "what goes up comes down." But if you are flying in an airplane the higher laws of aerodynamics supersede the law of gravity and you fly through the air without going down. However, if the engines stop functioning the lesser law of gravity takes over and the plane will come down.

We can see this principle in the prior verses (13-22) that stated there is a war going on between the flesh (our bent to please self rather than God) and our spirit; "For you, brethren, have been called to liberty; only do not *use* liberty as an opportunity for the flesh, but through love serve one another. For all the law is fulfilled in one word, *even* in this: "You shall love your neighbor as yourself." But if you bite and devour one another, beware lest you be consumed by one another! I say then: Walk in the Spirit, and you shall not fulfill the lust of the flesh. For the flesh lusts against the Spirit, and the Spirit against the flesh; and these are contrary to one another, Now the works of the flesh are evident, which are: adultery, fornication, uncleanness, lewdness, idolatry, sorcery, hatred, contentions, jealousies, outbursts of wrath, selfish ambitions, dissensions, heresies, envy, murders, drunkenness, revelries, and the like; of which I tell you beforehand, just as I also told *you* in time past, that those who practice such things will not inherit the kingdom of God."

Then we are told the law of the flesh can be overcome by operating in the higher law of walking in the Holy Spirit (the fruit of the Spirit). If you are not walking in the Spirit the lesser law of the flesh will prevail and you find yourself doing and acting in the ways of the flesh that make you miserable.

The first fruit listed is love for love is the supreme test of a believer, not his or her church membership, baptism, confirmation, church attendance, Bible study, prayer, or any such thing. The supreme test is whether or not he or she loves as God loves.

Seeing this principle I began to wonder what was keeping me from developing the first fruit listed—love. Immediately 1 John 4:18 came to my mind; "There is no fear in love; but perfect love casts out fear, because fear involves torment. But he who fears has not been made perfect in love." From this I began to look at the principle of fear and its warfare against love and other ways love is attacked, such as unforgiveness, envy, and hatred, and how love could be used as a weapon to overcome these and other attacks.

Joy is a word more often used than understood. To develop and use joy successfully in spiritual attacks requires the understanding it is not happiness. It is not an emotion or feeling, but a powerful spiritual force developed through praise and worship of God.

Happiness depends upon circumstances. If they are good you feel awesome and if they are bad you feel sad and depressed. Since joy is not an emotion it is not limited by good or bad circumstances and can overcome the emotional responses. Therefore we find in James 1:2 that joy is the way to overcome test and trials.

Jesus declares that in this world we will have tests and trials but to be of good joy as He has overcome the world. Test and trial can cause despair, depression, discouragement, and hopelessness. Joy will empower you to overcome theses and other attacks.

Peace is a state of quiet tranquility and freedom from disturbances and agitation. It is one of the most elusive conditions to mankind—but universally sought after. There is hardly a person, young or old, male or female, single or married that is not under some type of stress, it may come from a job, inflation, the home, relationship, or world conditions. This stress has resulted in worry, anxiety, tension, distress, and a host of similar maladies. The increase in drug sales to aid people under these stresses, the increases of patients in mental hospitals and under doctors' care clearly reveal the enemy is waging a fairly successful war.

The path to peace is taught in Philippians 4:5-6, "Be anxious for nothing, but in everything by prayer and supplication, with thanksgiving, let your requests be made known to God; 7 and the peace of God, which surpasses all understanding, will guard your hearts and minds through Christ Jesus."

The common thread in the first three fruits is our personal trust and faith in God. The next three, patience, gentleness, and goodness relate to how we treat one another.

Patience, longsuffering, endurance, and perseverance are all translation of the same Greek word. Endurance is probably the best word to convey the true meaning for us. It means the bearing of injuries or provocation for a long period and not being easily provoked by others' actions or inactivity. Long-suffering is one of the attributes that reveals the glory of God in Exodus 34:6.

Since patience is of God's nature we do not have to pray for it, as He does not have a thing called patience to give us. We need to pray for the grace to let His patience be developed in us as it is necessary to obtain the promises of God and experience what is legally ours.

Patience is developed through prayer, thanksgiving, and rejoicing. The enemies of patience are anger, strife, violence, impatience, and frustration, plus other weapons the enemy uses to keep us from our inheritances.

Our salvation, for example, is the result of God being patient with us, not desiring that any perish (2 Peter 3:9) However, those who never come to repentance demonstrate the truth that one may successfully resist God.

Gentleness is the next fruit and it is the ability to be mild, kind, yielding, and apt to give place. It is free from anything low and vulgar. It is developed through accepting imperfection in others.

A major weapon used to steal and destroy this fruit is irritation. To be irritated is to be provoked or exasperated. There are three main sources of irritation: people, environment, and self. The personality, traits, habits, and inconsideration of others provide an ever-present potential irritant. The deficiencies, inconveniences, and pressures of environment also provide sources of potential irritants. A third source is our own defects, weaknesses, and personal deficiencies.

King David said it was the gentleness of God that made him great. This implies that the correct response to an irritant is to discern how it can be used to develop godly character and conform us into the image of Jesus (Psalms 18:35)

Goodness is the fruit that reflects on God's attitude toward us and acts beneficially towards others. It is kind, merciful, compassionate, upright, gracious, pleasant, polite, cheerful, earnest, and moral. Some weapons used against goodness are rejection, failure, insecurity, and disappointment, designed to keep us from serving others.

Our life is to be a pattern of not just works but good works as commanded in Matthew 5:16, "Let your light so shine before men, that they may see your good works and glorify your Father in heaven." Good works are those that God has assigned us to complete.

The remaining three fruit—faith, meekness and self-control, involve our spiritual growth in trusting God's word, submitting to God's will, and the disciplining of our soul and body.

Because faith is so important I am going to look at it in more depth. Man's problem with faith is that since Adam ate of the fruit of the tree of knowledge of good and evil man has only used faith in the natural and physical realm. This has limited his ability to exercise faith to the realm of his five senses.

Some people have assumed that whenever faith is mentioned in Scripture, it is always talking about the same type of faith. This is not true. There are two types of faith—natural and spiritual and several kinds of faith, such as faith to live by, faith as a gift, and faith as a fruit.

It is in the natural realm that we first see the reality of faith operating in the physical and natural laws of the universe. The four seasons inform us that there is a time to sow and a time to reap. A farmer in Iowa will not plant his crops in the winter, for he knows he would not reap in the springtime. In the physical realm it is the law of gravity that keeps our feet on the ground. If someone decided to jump off a building, he would not fly like a bird; he would fall to the ground.

However, we know the law of gravity can be superseded by a higher law such as the higher law of aerodynamic, lift, and thrust, that allows airplanes to fly and astronauts to go far out into space beyond the force of gravity. However if the engines go out the lesser law of gravity would cause the airplane and space shuttle to fall to the ground.

Natural faith demonstrates how highly trained we are in our five senses of sight, touch, sound, smell, and taste. We exercise this faith without realizing it, as it requires no effort on our part. In exercising this faith we contradict the age-old adage—*I can't believe what I can't see.* We go up to a coke machine, put in our money, and make our selection. It never enters our minds that we might get a can of Pepsi if we select Coca-cola. Then we pull off the tab and take a big swallow without any worry or anxiety that we might be drinking poison. Yet, we had not seen the can or the contents before we exercised our natural faith and made our selection.

I find it amazing how well the five senses get along with one another? If you walk into a room where someone has on perfume, your nose would immediately inform you of the fact. Your eyes would not get upset and argue with your nose because they could not see the perfume. Your hands would not say, "I can't feel any perfume." Your ears would not say, "I can't hear any perfume." Your mouth would not say, "I can't taste any perfume." Each of your five senses would agree with the sense of smell. But if you hear or see spiritual faith, which I call our sixth sense, the five senses will ask all kinds of questions and introduce doubt that it happened.

I remember seeing for the first time people who had one leg shorter than the other being prayed over and the short leg grew to the same length of the other. My eyes said, "I saw it move." My mind said, "That's impossible it could not move." After seeing six legs grow my emotions were in turmoil that I had seen something that could not happen, happen.

There are also spiritual laws that govern the universe and they supersede the natural and physical laws as seen in Romans 8:2 that the law of the Spirit of life in Christ Jesus sets you free from the law of sin and death. This truth is also found in Galatians 5:16-18 and 23, where it is revealed that we can learn to live and walk in the law of the Spirit which will keep us free from the works of the flesh.

Below are a few contrasts of these laws to think upon:

> The law of the Spirit is *strength* and the law of sin is weakness.
> The law of the Spirit is *love* and the law of sin is selfishness.
> The law of the Spirit is *trust* and the law of sin is doubt.
> The law of the Spirit is *life* and the law of sin is death.
> The law of the Spirit is *health* and the law of sin is sickness and disease.
> The law of the Spirit is *prosperity* and the law of sin is poverty.

The law of the Spirit is *peace* and the law of sin is distress.

The law of the Spirit is *faith* and the law of sin is doubt and unbelief.

The Bible also reveals several blessings of the law of faith:

Ephesians 2:8	Saved through faith
Romans 5:1	Justified by faith
Galatians 5:5	Righteousness by faith
Romans 1:17	Live by faith
11 Corinthians 5:7	Walk by faith
Acts 26:18	Sanctified by faith
Acts 15:9	Purify hearts by faith
1 John 5:4	Overcome world by faith
Acts 14:9	Healed by faith
11 Corinthians 1:24	Stand by faith
1 Timothy 3:13	Great boldness by faith
Hebrews 6:12	Inherit promises by faith
Hebrews 10:22	Draw near to God by Faith
1 Peter 5:9	Resist the devil by faith

I could go on, for the Scriptures I have listed do not exhaust all that faith enables us to be and do. They do, however, show that spiritual faith is not mental faith. It is not something that can be grasped by the emotions and intellect. In fact, as we have noted, the opposite is true. Our minds and emotions war against faith, for they are limited by the five senses until we receive the faith of Jesus.

Meekness is submitting to the divine will of God rather than being proud and self-sufficient. To be meek is to be of soft temper, gentle, humble, yielding and forbearing under injury; not easily provoked. If God were not meek He would be unable to forbear our ill treatment and provocation of Him. Instead of being kind and gentle to us He would retaliate and punish us.

We are commanded in II Timothy 2:25 to be meek in instructing others who are opposing themselves. The problem we get into is trying to guide and teach those who are not meek but proud and arrogant. In so doing, we are attempting to do something even God does not do. Then, we get upset over our inability to teach them and for allowing them to provoke us. In my early years I would start out with the good intentions of helping someone and wind up in an argument or some type of disagreement. Once my emotions got involved forbearance went out the window and I lost the opportunity to show meekness to the one in need.

On the other hand is our attitude when God is trying to guide and teach us. Many times we cannot receive from others because we are not humble and meek. We think too highly of ourselves and question how a person of lesser rank could possibly teach us anything. Meekness allows us to esteem our brother more highly than ourselves and to prefer him above ourselves. It is the opposite of pride, which exalts self and shows contempt for others. Therefore we are commanded in James 1:21 to receive instruction with meekness.

Another issue in desiring to instruct others is a tendency to carry a false burden and responsibility for God's glory and reputation. As we saw with Eve, the moment Satan seduced her into defending God she went beyond God's instruction. God had said not to eat of the Tree of Knowledge of Good and Evil, and Eve added that they were not to touch the tree.

There is also a tendency to forget that the Tree of Knowledge is both good and evil, and to think of it as only evil. In so doing, we are open to the deception that good knowledge will change us or someone else. The Bible is the Word of God, but the Bible is not to take the place of the Lord Himself, or the Holy Spirit who convicts, give repentance, and lead us into truth. Knowing Scripture is not our goal, the goal is to know the Lord the Scripture reveals.

This was the deception of the religious people when Jesus was among them as a man. Jesus admonished them, "You search the Scriptures because you think that in them you have eternal life; but it is these that bear witness of Me" (John 5:39).

It is not my responsibility to teach but to allow the Holy Spirit to teach through me. Nor is it my responsibility to put the law into the minds and hearts of others. God does that when He puts His Spirit within them. What then is my responsibility toward others? It is to reveal Jesus unto them as no one can see Jesus and remain unchanged (II Corinthians 3:14-16)

It is the revelation of Jesus that our Father uses to subdue us. When we see Jesus, we are consumed by His worthiness, His lovingness, His beautifulness, His holiness, and His glory, power, and majesty. The revelation of Jesus takes us beyond redemption, beyond the gifts of the Spirit, beyond the blessings, beyond the work that must be done, into fellowship with Him.

One of the many benefits from coming into fellowship with God is the laying down of all false responsibilities that burden us with so much work, so much worry, so much anxiety, so much fear of failure, so much fear of rejection. It is not our responsibility to make people obey.

The ultimate responsibility for salvation, holiness, truth, or any other need someone might have is not with us, but with God. Every believer is a priest unto God and must hear God for himself. Although we are responsible to teach and instruct with all meekness those who are opposing themselves, we are not to stand in the place of God.

The last fruit we shall study is a Biblical word translated *temperance* and can mean strength, self-control, and soberness. Self-control is the preferable rendering, as temperance is now limited to the idea of moderation as opposed to excess.

Control denotes power, authority, government, and command. To control is to check or restrain, to overpower, to direct or govern in opposition, to have superior force or authority over, to have under command. The various powers bestowed by God upon man are capable of being abused therefore the right use of these powers demands the controlling power of the Holy Spirit.

In Acts 24:25, temperance follows "righteousness" representing God's claims, with self-control being man's response. In II Peter 1:6, temperance follows "knowledge," implying that revelation is to be put into practice.

Temperance or self-control is the power to check restrain and govern our life according to God's will. It is a powerful spiritual force that enables us to discipline our soul and body to produce a godly lifestyle. We need this grace because only our spirit has been recreated and Satan and sin still have access to our soul and body making us subject to spiritual warfare. As we saw in the study of the Evil Empire Satan will use every device of the world to bring us back into captivity and bondage of sin.

Some of the weapons used in the warfare are lust, emotions, and our mind. *Lust* is an eagerness to possess or enjoy that which the spirit, soul, and body desire. It may be godly or ungodly. To lust after God and have a longing desire to be like Jesus is godly. To lust after carnal pleasure and long to enjoy unlawful affections and desires is ungodly.

There is a tendency for us to think of lust in terms of sensuality and sexual desires. This is only one way in which lust operates. We also have desires to possess various things—money, power, status, wisdom, food, clothes, cars, and other things of the world. And we are told in James 1:13-15 that it is our own lust that gives birth to sin.

Because we are selfish creatures many times we will please self even to our own hurt. For it is the nature of lust to desire to please self, even at the expense of God and others. Each of us must face this godless side of our nature and learn to win in this warfare. If we do not, our lust will conceive and bring forth sin, and sin will bring forth death.

Think again about Adam and Eve in the garden. They were given every pleasure, every delight, everything necessary for the good life, yet they still wanted more. They lusted to be more than creatures; they wanted to be gods.

There are three areas of intense lustful warfare—money, power, and sex. Throughout history, money manifests itself as power and sex is used to acquire both money and power. These three subjects are spoken of more frequently in the Bible than other areas of warfare. Yet there are other desires that can snare us. Everyone, for example, gets hungry and could be snared by gluttony or some other extreme use of food and drink. We can also lust for things that we feel will make us more comfortable, give us more pleasure, or make us more acceptable. We can lust for various drugs such as alcohol, cocaine, and nicotine. Regardless of how the warfare of lust might come, the principles will be the same.

Keep in mind that in our study of the world, we saw that Satan has organized a system to rule over us. We must, therefore, constantly remind ourselves that friendship with the world makes us enemies of God. One of the most powerful tools of the world, which Satan uses to rule us, is money.

Jesus understood this warfare and spoke about money more frequently than any other subject except the Kingdom of God such as:

- Luke 16:13, ""No servant can serve two masters; for either he will hate the one and love the other, or else he will be loyal to the one and despise the other. You cannot serve God and mammon."
- Matthew 6; 19-21, "Do not lay up for yourselves treasures on earth, where moth and rust destroy and where thieves break in and steal; 20 but lay up for yourselves treasures in heaven, where neither moth nor rust destroys and where thieves do not break in and steal. 21 For where your treasure is, there your heart will be also."
- 1 Timothy 6:10, " For the love of money is the root of all evil: which while some coveted after, they have erred from the faith, and pierced themselves through with many sorrows."

These statements about money do not line up with what some have been taught about living an abundant life. There are many people, who think money is a sign of God's blessing, and hence poverty a sign of God's displeasure.

Very few ever think of money as having an evil force, so if Satan can deceive one into thinking that money is an impersonal medium of exchange rather than a power seeking to dominate they can be snared by the lust for money.

I have written a three volume series, "How To Win In Spiritual Warfare," that explores in more detail how to develop each of the nine fruit and use them as spiritual weapons. If you are interested or desire more information on these studies visit my web site joesmithministries.net

ELEVEN

How Does It All End?

There are many books and articles on last days' prophecies, and so many signs that point to the soon return of Jesus that it would be too much of an undertaking for me to cover them in this chapter. So I will provide what I think are some very important ones.

Jesus said there would be wars and rumors of wars; kingdoms will rise against kingdoms, and nations against nations. (Matthew 24:6-7) If you read the newspapers or watch the news on TV, you know that all over the world this is happening.

There are also the signs of famine, earthquakes, floods, and droughts. I live in Florida, and we have indeed had our share of natural disasters of hurricanes and tornadoes, but nothing compared to Katrina in New Orleans.

Another end time sign is the spirit of lawlessness. With the redefining of the word "tolerance" and what is right and wrong, we should not be surprised that people are doing what is right in their own eyes and not God's.

The Apostle Paul wrote about this in II Timothy 3:1-5, "But know this, that in the last days perilous times will come: For men will be lovers of themselves, lovers of money, boasters, proud, blasphemers, disobedient to parents, unthankful, unholy, unloving, unforgiving, slanderers, without self-control, brutal, despisers of good, traitors, headstrong, haughty, lovers of pleasure rather than lovers of God, having a form of godliness but denying its power. And from such people turn away!"

Notice that he addressed people who have a form of godliness. The sad truth is that many men who oversee churches and claim to be men of God do not preach the Word of God. Nor do they believe what God states about Jesus' resurrection, Satan, heaven and hell, or the Lordship of Jesus, as they, too, are doing what is right in their own eyes.

We are told in Romans 6:23 that the wages of sin is death, but the power of the gospel is eternal life through the gift of Jesus. Therefore, if this gospel does not have the power to change a person from being a lover of self and living in sin to being a lover of God, it does not have the power to save you. The passage from II Timothy ends with a commandment to turn away from people who have a form of godliness but deny its power.

I have wondered how the signs in Revelation about the end times could ever happen. We are told there will be a one-world government ruled by a false prophet who derives his power from a beast, and no one can buy or sell without the mark of the beast. Then there are the two witnesses of Christ who are killed and left lying in the street for three and a half days and later come to life, and the entire world will see it (Revelation 13:17 and 11:3-13)

With the advancement of knowledge, we can now see possibilities that a few years ago seemed impossible. Peter spoke of the earth being purged and cleansed by fire and the elements melting (2 Peter 3:12). Nuclear energy demonstrates this can happen. Furthermore, through computers and satellites one can access the entire world. Satellite technology exists today that can zoom in on your street and house and read the license plate on your automobile. This indicates to me people all over the world can and will witness two men lying dead in the street. computers and satellites have also made a one-world government possible and with all types of trading taking place it soon will be possible for governments to control the world's economy.

The Lord has given us signs so that none would perish but all come to repentance (2 Peter 3:9). My question for you is, "Are you prepared for Jesus' return? Will He come as your Lord and Savior or as your Judge?" He will be one or the other. There are no other options.

At the age of 45, our second son Jeff was killed on a rainy night in a one-car accident on his way home. He left behind a wife and five children. When others learned I was going to officiate his funeral, some had a hard time believing I could do it. After all, this was my son, and the death of a loved one is usually defined as an emotional and devastating event. This prompted me to stop and consider that the church has failed to prepare believers for an unavoidable event: If you are alive, it is 100% certain you will die.

Another sad truth is that many truly born-again, loving Jesus Christians are clueless about the future simply because they are not taught what happens after death, except that a person goes to either heaven or hell. And about the only time they hear of heaven and hell is at funerals.

It breaks my heart to think that Christians have no Biblical truths of what their life after death will be like. Consequently they live a life without purpose or meaning—go to work, go home, raise children, retire, and then die. Some even go to church, but have no assurance their sins have been forgiven or if they die they will go to heaven. Most are also clueless about life on a new earth. I call this a "hope so religion" rather than a "know so religion"

Have you ever wondered why, if Christians really believe heaven is such a wonderful place, they are not happy and excited about going there? There are some Muslims who are so excited about heaven they are willing to be a kamikaze for their religion due to their leaders promise that the merciless act of blowing themselves up to kill others will guarantee a spot in heaven. I must admit I am not too impressed with those leaders as I know they are not absolutely sure they are going to heaven and wonder if heaven is guaranteed why are they not the first ones to blow themselves up.

In fact, you can already see a stark contrast between Christianity and Islam through their leadership. The Muslim leaders challenge their followers to prove their love for Allah by blowing themselves up. Jesus, on the other hand said I am going to prove my love for you by going to the cross and dying for you and ask that we prove our love for him by obeying His commandments.

We as Christians have a guarantee through the resurrection of Jesus that we will go to heaven as the Apostle Paul reveals in 1 Corinthians 15:51-58, "Behold, I show you a mystery; we shall not all sleep, but we shall all be changed, in a moment, in the twinkling of an eye, at the last trump: for the trumpet shall sound, and the dead shall be raised incorruptible, and we shall be changed. For this corruptible must put on incorruption, and this mortal must put on immortality. So when this corruptible shall have put on incorruption, and this mortal shall have put on immortality, then shall be brought to pass the saying that is written, death is swallowed up in victory. 0 death, where is thy sting? 0 grave, where is thy victory? The sting of death is sin; and the strength of sin is the law. But thanks be to God, which gives us the victory through our Lord Jesus Christ. Therefore, my beloved brethren, be ye steadfast, unmovable, always abounding in the work of the Lord, forasmuch, as ye know that your labor is not in vain in the Lord."

Until Jesus was resurrected the devil used death as a powerful weapon of fear but now we know death is not an enemy to fear but a blessing to give us victory and a new life. The Apostle Paul reveals to us that physical death is not an end but a beginning of a new life free from the curse of sin and will never die again. So death is a means by which God transitions us from our corruptible flesh to incorruption, and from our mortal body to immortality.

The last verse in this passage makes a startling statement; "Therefore, my beloved brethren, be ye steadfast, unmovable, always abounding in the work of the Lord, forasmuch, as ye know that your labor is not in vain in the Lord." There are two reasons for being steadfast, unmovable, and always abounding in the work of the Lord. First is the reality that after death comes two judgments. One is called the "White Throne Judgment" and the other the "Judgment Seat of Christ."

Anyone whose name is not written in the Lamb's Book of Life because they have not been born again by the Spirit of God will face the White Throne Judgment. The Judgment Seat of Christ is for Christians who must give an account for their stewardship over the gifting of God and the fulfilling of His plans and purposes for creating them.

Here is some good and bad news. The good news is that there is life after death. This may surprise you, but heaven is not our final destination. Christians will not live for eternity in heaven but on a new earth. The bad news is that if a Christian has not been steadfast, unmovable, and abounding in the work of the Lord, he will only be rewarded with life on the new earth.

Let me give you a Scriptural basis for what I am teaching you. When God created the earth, He created it for His family. He declared everything He created was good and for the pleasure of His family. The sin of Adam and Eve did not change God's plan to have a family living on earth. Their sin separated them from God and put the earth and all of creation under the curse of death, corruption, and entropy. It also gave Satan legal authority to rule.

As we have seen, Satan rules on earth through a system the Bible calls the world. Thus the world has an evil mind behind it. This is why government, education, arts, business, and just about everything in the world, have a propensity towards evil and why God commands us to not love the world.

In Revelation 11:15, we are told this good news: "Then the seventh angel sounded: And there were loud voices in heaven, saying, 'The kingdoms of this world have become the kingdoms of our Lord and of His Christ, and He shall reign forever and ever!'" One day the reign of Satan on earth will cease and there will only be one ruler-Jesus-and one kingdom-the kingdom of God. Thus, Jesus is coming back to earth again to remove Satan and all wickedness and to restore the earth to God's family.

Act 1:1-7 records that Jesus spent forty days with the disciples teaching them about things pertaining to the kingdom of God, "The former account I made, 0 Theophilus, of all that Jesus began both to do and teach, until the day in which He was taken up, after He through the Holy Spirit had given commandments to the apostles whom He had chosen, to whom He also presented Himself alive after His suffering by many infallible proofs, being seen by them during forty days and speaking of the things pertaining to the kingdom of God. And being assembled together with them, He commanded them not to depart from Jerusalem, but to wait for the Promise of the Father, "which," He said, "you have heard from Me; for John truly baptized with water, but you shall be baptized with the Holy Spirit not many days from now." Therefore, when they had come together, they asked Him, saying, "Lord, will You at this time restore thc kingdom to Israel?" And He said to them, "It is not for you to know times or seasons which the Father has put in His own authority."

Did you notice that when the disciples asked Jesus the question about ruling, He did not say they had incorrect ideas, or that He was not going to rule as they thought? His answer was that this was not the time and only the Father knew when the time would come.

I would love to have that tape series on Jesus' teachings concerning the Kingdom. But the only things revealed to us is that He told the disciples about the baptism in the Holy Spirit, the power to witness, and that Jesus is going to come again to planet earth.

It seems to me that most sermons and books about His return address the presence or absence of the rapture and tribulation for the church rather than what will happen when He returns. The good news is that we have many Scriptures in both the Old and New Testaments that reveal what will happen when He returns.

At times, Jesus used parables when speaking of the kingdom, and told the disciples that He did this so they would know and understand the mysteries of the kingdom. We have one of these in Luke 19:11-27, "As they heard these things, He spoke another parable, because He was near Jerusalem and because they thought the kingdom of God would appear immediately. Therefore He said: "A certain nobleman went into a far country to receive for himself a kingdom and to return. So he called ten of his servants, delivered to them ten minas, and said to them, 'Do business till I come.' But his citizens hated him, and sent a delegation after him, saying, 'We will not have this man to reign over us.' And so it was that when he returned, having received the kingdom, he then commanded these servants, to whom he had given the money, to be called to him, that he might know how much every man had gained by trading. Then came the first, saying, 'Master, your mina has earned ten minas.' And he said to him, 'Well done, good servant; because you were faithful in a very little, have authority over ten cities.' And the second came, saying, 'Master, your mina has earned five minas.' Likewise he said to him, 'You also be over five cities.' Then another came, saying, 'Master, here is your mina, which I have kept put away in a handkerchief. For I feared you, because you are an austere man. You collect what you did not deposit, and reap what you did not sow.' And he said to him, 'Out of your own mouth I will judge you, you wicked servant. You knew that I was an austere man, collecting what I did not deposit, and reaping what I did not sow. Why then did you not put my money in the bank, that at my coming I might have collected it with interest?' And he said to those who stood by, 'Take the mina from him, and give it to him who has ten minas.' (But they said to him, 'Master, he has ten minas.') For I say to you, that to everyone who has will be given; and from him who does not have, even what he has will be taken away from him. But bring here those enemies of mine, who did not want me to reign over them, and slay them before me.'"

Here we see Jesus and the disciples were approaching Jerusalem, the capital city of Israel, and the question was again raised about His earthly kingdom. He now answers in a different manner because they did not know His spiritual kingdom must first be established on earth before His earthly kingdom could be established.

Jesus tells them of a ruler giving money and then going away to receive the kingdom, and then returning. Those who had increased their money were rewarded with being rulers over cities and entering into his joy. This tells me that when Jesus' earthly kingdom comes He will give those who are ready work to do in His kingdom. So we need to be using the gifts Jesus has given us to increase and be ready to serve when He sets up His earthly kingdom.

In both texts, we find the disciples understood Jesus, as the Messiah, was to occupy the throne of David and rule over Israel and the world. So they wanted to know when He was going to bring this about. They had good reason to believe and inquire about this from the revelation in Luke 1:31-33 where the angel Gabriel told Mary, "And behold, you will conceive in your womb and bring forth a Son, and shall call His name Jesus. He will be great, and will be called the Son of the Highest; and the Lord God will give Him the throne of His father David. And He will reign over the house of Jacob forever, and of His kingdom there will be no end."

We find Peter further declaring that the prophets and the angels also desired to look into the subject of salvation in 1 Peter 1:10-13, "Of which salvation the prophets have enquired and searched diligently, who prophesied of the grace that should come unto you: Searching what, or what manner of time the Spirit of Christ which was in them did signify, when it testified beforehand the sufferings of Christ, and the glory that should follow. Unto whom it was revealed, that not unto themselves, but unto us they did minister the things, which are now reported unto you by them that have preached the gospel unto you with the Holy Ghost sent down from heaven; which things the angels desire to look into." We now know the spiritual kingdom is the church and the people of the spiritual kingdom are the ones who have been born again through Jesus.

The establishing of Jesus earthly kingdom has two phases. The first phase takes place when Jesus enters into Jerusalem and reigns for one thousand years as foretold in Revelation 20:1-7, "I saw an angel coming down from heaven, having the key to the bottomless pit and a great chain in his hand. He laid hold of the dragon, that serpent of old, who is the Devil and Satan, and bound him for a thousand years; and he cast him into the bottomless pit, and shut him up, and set a seal on him, so that he should deceive the nations no more till the thousand years were finished. But after these things he must be released for a little while. And I saw thrones, and they sat on them, and judgment was committed to them. Then I saw the souls of those who had been beheaded for their witness to Jesus and for the word of God, who had not worshiped the beast or his image, and had not received his mark on their foreheads or on their hands. And they lived and reigned with Christ for a thousand years. But the rest of the dead did not live again until the thousand years were finished. This is the first resurrection. Blessed and holy is he who has part in the first resurrection. Over such the second death has no power, but they shall be priests of God and of Christ, and shall reign with Him a thousand years."

Here we are told the Devil will be bound up during the thousand-year reign. Since the Devil and demons are bound up, there will be no wars, and no sickness and disease, so life will be prolonged. Isaiah Chapter Eleven and other books (Daniel, Jeremiah, Ezekiel and Zechariah) reveal that this will be a time of prosperity, peace, harmony, and long life. People will live to be one hundred years old and be perceived as a child. Children will play next to poisonous serpents and not be bitten. The lamb will lie down with the lion and not be eaten. There will be an abundance of rain and sunlight with a seven-fold increase of light. This will cause the wilderness to blossom as a rose and it will produce the greatest production of every crop and fruit that has ever been known.

This revelation of the thousand-year reign of Jesus gives us just a little glimpse into what the new heaven and new earth will be like. (Contrast this description to the sin-cursed earth and one world government Satan will establish.)

During the thousand-year reign, the seat of government will be Jerusalem and Jesus will rule with a rod of iron. Thus the people who are living on earth at this time will not be permitted to do evil acts (Revelation 19:15)

However, Zechariah 14:16-18 tells us there will be those living at this time who will refuse to go up to Jerusalem to worship Jesus, "And it shall come to pass, that every one that is left of all the nations which came against Jerusalem shall even go up from year to year to worship the King, the LORD of hosts, and to keep the feast of tabernacles. And it shall be, that whoso will not come up of all the families of the earth unto Jerusalem to worship the King, the LORD of hosts, even upon them shall be no rain. And if the family of Egypt go not up, and come not, that have no rain; there shall be the plague, wherewith the LORD will smite the heathen that come not up to keep the feast of tabernacles."

From this passage we learn why the rule of Jesus is to be a rule of iron: some people will have a rebellious spirit and will not want Jesus to rule over them. This truth is further revealed by what happens next according to Revelation 20:7-10, "Now when the thousand years have expired, Satan will be released from his prison and will go out to deceive the nations which are in the four comers of the earth, Gog and Magog, to gather them together to battle, whose number is as the sand of the sea. They went up on the breadth of the earth and surrounded the camp of the saints and the beloved city. And fire came down from God out of heaven and devoured them. The devil, which deceived them, was cast into the lake of fire and brimstone where the beast and the false prophet are. And they will be tormented day and night forever and ever."

When the Devil is loosed from the pit for a season he will rally those rebellious ones to join him in overthrowing God's government. They will gladly do so, as they are tired of the rule of iron that kept them from doing wicked and evil things. Thus, they will demonstrate beyond any doubt there are those who will refuse to obey and serve God under the best of circumstances, and will go to Jerusalem to overthrow the government of God. But just as the devil lost in his attempt to take over heaven he now looses his final attempt to take back Jesus kingdom on earth. At this time, God will decree that time has expired for the Devil and all those who oppose Him, for God will have given man every chance possible to worship Him. There will be nothing else for God to do, so the end will come and man will have no more opportunities to repent and acknowledge Jesus as their Lord. Then the White Throne Judgment will occur, where all those who refused to worship, honor, and obey God will be judged and cast into hell. They will be separated from God forever and ever.

To give you a better understanding of sinners being kept in Hades until they are thrown into hell after the White Throne Judgment think of a criminal being kept in jail (a place of torment) until he goes before a judge. The judge declares him guilty and he goes from jail to prison that is worse than jail.

The second phase of establishing Jesus earthly kingdom comes next when God will create the new heaven and the new earth to be what He planned from the very beginning of creation. He will be God and we will be His people living on a perfect planet in perfect harmony with Him and all creation (Revelation 20: 11 through 21:4)

With regards to the new earth, let's begin with the vegetable kingdom. The colors we now see in the flowers, trees, and shrubs are beautiful, but they are imperfect due to sin. In the new earth, their colors will be so perfect and intense; you will stand in awe at their magnificence. In the new earth, crops will grow abundantly, as the ground is no longer cursed and there is plenty of rain. Thus there will be no famine or hunger as we see in many parts of the world today. No sun or moon will exist, as the Lord will be our light. Therefore, we will see the sky in all its beauty. There will be no fear or hostility among the animals and humans, and we will once again be able to communicate with them just as Adam and Eve did in the beginning.

And what will you be doing? Exactly what God created you to do. So your task will be pleasurable, not dreadful. This is why you should now be doing the works God created you to do and getting ready for the future. After all, you are not going to spend eternity floating around on a cloud bored to tears. Your co-workers and your boss will also be in perfect harmony with God and with you. They will not be jealous, or envious, or giving you a hard time.

Furthermore on this new earth there will be no room for hate, anger, violence, murder, war, sickness, disease, deformities, death, or evil of any kind forever and ever as the curse of sin will no longer exist.

If you are interested in an awesome discourse on this subject, I recommend the book by Randy Alcorn, *Heaven,* ©2004 by Eternal Perspective Ministries.

You may be asking what you need to do to make sure you have a future that holds nothing but good for you. The answer is to repent. This means you make a decision to change your thoughts with regards to Jesus. Here is how the Holy Spirit explains it in Romans 10:7-11, "The word is near you, in your mouth and in your heart (that is, the word of faith which we preach): that if you confess with your mouth the Lord Jesus and believe in your heart that God has raised Him from the dead, you will be saved. For with the heart one believes unto righteousness, and with the mouth confession is made unto salvation. For the Scripture says, "Whoever believes on Him will not be put to shame.""

On the other hand, if you die without your name being written in the Lamb's Book of Life, your future is horrible. You will never know or experience what it is like to be truly loved and accepted for who you are and not what you can do. You will never have the joy and blessing of knowing God, your Creator, or why you were born into this world. You will be forever separated from God and just as you have never found fulfillment in this life, you will never find it in the next life, as it can only be found through Jesus now and forever.

Keep in mind there is no Scripture that implies when you die you will instantly become more spiritually mature than you were at death. In the new earth, you will begin your journey at whatever level you had achieved during this life.

Are you ready?